15

GRAMMA

FOR ALL

GRAMMAR FOR ALL

Sabri Kamel

B.A., P.T.C.

DARF PUBLISHERS LTD
LONDON

Printed in Great Britain by A. Wheaton & Co. Ltd, Exeter

CONTENTS

A SENTENCE الجملة

A sentence is a group of words that makes complete sense. **الجملة هي مجموعة كلمات تعطينا معنى كاملا**

Predicate وجزء متعلق به **Subject** وتتكون من فاعل

Example	Subject	Predicate
1.	The sun	shines.
2.	Hard-working boys	usually succeed.
3.	He	gave me a book.

تلاحظ في المثال الثاني ان الفاعل قد يكون موصوفا ٠
والفاعل قد يكون اسمًا noun كالمثال الاول والثاني وقد يكــون
ضميرا Pronoun ويستعمل بدلا من الاسم لتحاشي التكرار

PRONOUNS الضمائــر

Number	Subject فاعل		Object مفعول به		Possessive ملكية	
Singular مفرد	I	أنا	me	ـني	my, mine	ملكي
	You	أنت	you	ـك	your, yours	ملكك
	He	هو	him	ـه	his, his	ملكه
	She	هي	her	ـها	her, hers	ملكها
	It	هو او هي لغير العاقل	it	ـه	its, its.	ملكه
plural جمع	They	هم	us	نا	our, ours	ملكنا
	We	نحن	you	كم	your, yours	ملككم
	You	أنتم	them	ـهم	their, theirs	ملكهم

Examples:-

1. **I** have a book. **It** is **my** book. **It** is **mine.**
2. **You** have a book. **It** is **your** book. **It** is **yours.**
3. **He** has a book. **It** is **his** book. **It** is **his.**
4. **She** has a book. **It** is **her** book. **It** is **hers.**
5. **We** have book. **They** are **our** books. **They** are **ours.**

6. **You** have books. They are **your** books. They are **yours**.

7. **They** have books. They are **their** books. They are **theirs**.

8. **I** saw **him**. رأيته   9. He saw **me**. رآني

10. **We** talked to **them**. تحدثنا اليهم

11. **I** trust **you**. أثق فيك

12. **We** believed **her**. صدقناها

13. **They** played with **us**. لعبوا معنا

ARTICLES   الادوات

A or An معناهما (واحد) ولذلك فانهما تسبقان الاسماء المفردة
An egg   :   A book مثل فقط (indefinite)

١ ـ **An** تسبق الاسماء المفردة المبتدئة بأحد الحروف المتحركـــة
An apple, an egg.   مثل **A, E, I, O, U.** الآتية

٢ ـ **A** تسبق كل اسم مفرد غير مبتدىء بأحد الحروف السابقــة
A cat, a girl مثل

٣ ـ تستعمل **The** للدلالة على المعرفة (definite) وتسبق الكلمات
The boys, The boy المفردة والجمع سواء مذكر او مؤنث مثل

EXERCISE 1

Put a or an in the space:-

1. ...... fly
2. ...... ink
3. ...... boy
4. ...... invitation
5. ...... order

ملحوظة : (١) لا تستعمل **The** في الحالات الآتية :
١ ـ أسماء **الجمع النكرة** مثل Boys - Girls
٢ ـ **الاسماء المعنوية** مثل الجبن cowardice الشجاعة courage
الجمال beauty

٣ ـ الاسماء التي تدل علــى **مواد** مثل water الماء wood **الخشب**
(٢) لا تستعمل a أو an مـــع أسماء المدن مثل Cairo

الافعال المساعدة   Helping Verbs

(a) «Verb **to Be»**   am, is, are, was, were.

تستعمل am مع I في الزمـــن المضارع I am a clever boy
تستعمل is مع المفرد في الزمن المضارع He is a clever boy
تستعمل are مع الجمع في الزمن المضارع We are in the class
وتستعمل was مـــع المفرد في الزمن الماضي
وتستعمل were مع الجمع في الزمن الماضي

Ex. 2. Fill in the spaces using **am, is** or **are**:-
    1. **I** .... in the classroom.
    2. **She** .... cooking food.
    3. **You** .... clever boys.
    4. **They** .... going to the cinema.
    5. **He** .... writing a letter.

(b) «Verb **to Have»**

للمفرد والجمع **تستعمل**   have
تستعمل **has** مع he **أو** she   أو it
تستعمل **had** في الماضي مفرد أو جمع

Ex: I have a book.
    He has a book.
    They have books.

Ex. 3. Fill in the space using **have** or **has**:-
    1. The dog ...... a tail.
    2. The boy ...... a bag.
    3. They ...... a house.
    4. I ...... ten fingers.
    5. Mary ...... a cat.

(c) **We** أو **I** مع المتكلم Shall تستعمل

We shall come to school.

تستعمل **will** مع باقي الضمائر

They will play football

would   **should**   وفي الماضي تستعمل

Ex. 4:- Fill in the spaces using «shall» or «will»

     1. I ...... throw the ball.

     2. You ...... run and get the ball.

     3. We ...... stand in the classroom.

     4. Farouk .... smell the rose.

     5. Farouk and Huda .... read this book.

(d) Verb To Do   **Do, Does, Did**

في المضارع   Do   تستعمل

في المضارع مع المفرد الغائب   Does   تستعمل

في الماضي   Did   تستعمل

Ex. 5. Fill in the spaces using «Do» or «Does»:-

     1. ...... you hear me ?

     2. ...... she cook food ?

     3. I ...... my work.

     4. ...... he pay attention ?

     5. ...... they read books ?

وهناك أفعال مساعدة أخرى مثل

may	يمكن	might	أمكن
can	يستطيع	could	استطاع
must	يجب	ought	كان من الواجب

قاعدة : يجب ان تشتمل كـل جملة في اللغـة الانجليزية على فعــل فاذا لــم يكــن هنــاك فعــل فــلا بــد أن نضع فعلا من الافعال المساعدة .

TENSES الازمنة

1. Present Simple Tense: المضارع البسيط

Fact ١ ـ يدل على عادة او حقيقة Habit

٢ ـ يأخذ الفعل المضارع حرف «S» مع it ,she, he,

أو المفرد الغائب مثـــل Mary, Ali, the girl, the boy

٣ ـ نضع الفعل في الزمن المضارع اذا أتت في الجملة كلمـــة من
الكلمات الآتية :

always دائما	often غالبا	usually عادة
sometimes وأحيانا	every كل	generally عادة

ملحوظة : توضع to قبل الفعل أحيانا لتبين أن الفعل نـم
يوضع بعــد في الزمن المناسب ولذلك يجب حذفهــا عنــد تصحيح
الافعال .

Example :

1. The cow (to give) us milk.
2. Ali (go) to the cinema every week.
(1) The cow gives us milk.
(2) Ali goes to the cinema every week.

Ex: 6. Put the Verbs in the correct tense:- صحح الافعال

1. We usually (to spend) summer at Ras-El-Bar.
2. He always (do) his exercises without making any mistake.
3. Sometimes, when a soldier (march) he (do) without water.
4. Boys generally (go) to school early.
5. In summer days (be) long but in winter they (be) short.
6. They always (pass) their holiday by the seaside.
7. The moon sometimes (shine) at night.
8. We often (go) to the cinema on Fridays.

9. My mother always (help) me when I (ask) her.

10. Every day we (leave) home at 7 o'clock.

11. It (rain) here in winter.

---

2. Past Simple Tense.   الماضي البسيط

١ ـ يــدل عـلى حــدث في الزمن   It shows a past action
الماضي .

٢ ـ يتحول الفعــل الى ماضي باضافة   **ed**
الى نهاية المصدر مثل   play   تصبح   played
وهناك بعض الافعال الشاذة يجب حفظها

٣ ـ نضع الفعل في الزمن الماضي اذا أتت في الجمـــــلة احدى
الكلمات الآتية : ـ

الماضي   last   منذ   **Ago**   أمس   Yesterday

Ex. 7. Correct these verbs: صحح هذه الافعال

1. We (to make) a journey to Alex. last summer.

2. I (to buy) a book yesterday.

3. The merchant (to sell) vegetables last year.

4. They (to play) football well two days ago.

5. We (succeed) last year.

6. Last week I (to see) him at Tanta and he (to ask) me some questions about my father who (to be) ill.

7. Three days ago I (to go) to meet my brother who (to want) to see me.

8. My friend was angry with me because I not (to visit) him when he (to be) ill.

9. Yesterday I (to find) a boy weeping in the street.

10. Ali (forgive) you yesterday.

3. Future   المستقبل

١ ــ يتكون من الفعل + **will**   أو   **Shall**

٢ ــ تأتي **shall**   مع ضمير المتكلم   **I & we**

٣ ــ تأتي **will**   مع باقي الضمائر

٤ ــ نضع الفعل في الزمن المستقبل اذا أتت احدى الكلمات الآتية :

في المستقبل **in future** التالي **next** غـــدا **To-morrow**

Example:-

1. I (to come) to school to-morrow.
2. They will play the next time.
1. I shall come to school to-morrow.
2. They will play the next time.

Ex. 8. Correct these verbs :   صحح هذه الافعال : ــ

1. They (to read) a book to-morrow.
2. We (to learn) French in future.
3. I (go) to Zagazig to-morrow.
4. We (give) him a book next week.
5. I (visit) the zoo to-morrow.

---

4. Present Continuous Tense   المضارع المستمر

١ ــ يتكون من : ing + **الفعل** + **am, is, are**

٢ ــ تأتي am   مع **I**

٣ ــ تأتي is   مع **المفرد**

٤ ــ تأتي are   مع **الجمع**

نضع الفعل في الزمن المضارع المستمر اذا أتت احدى الكلمـــات الآتية :

في الوقت الحاضر at the present time   الآن **Now**

في هذه اللحظة   at this moment

They (to read) the story **now.**

They **are reading** the story now.

Ex. 9. **Put the verb in the brackets in the right form :**

1. What she (do) now ? She (make) a new dress now.
2. What they (do) now ? They (write) an exercise now.
3. My mother (cook) the food in this moment.
4. Some boys (to play) in the garden now.
5. I (to write) now.
6. The farmer (sow) the seeds at this moment.
7. He (to play) with his ball now.
8. I (to answer) the teacher's questions now.
9. Now my father (build) a house at Giza.
10. Where your brother (go) now ?

5. Past Continuous Tense الماضي المستمر

١ ـ يتكون من + ing + الفعل + were أو was
٢ ـ يدل على حدث كان مستمرا في الزمن الماضي ثم قطعه حدث آخر

القاعدة : نضع الفعل الـذي يأتي بعد كلمتي as, while
مباشرة في الزمن الماضي المستمر ونضع باقي أفعال الجمـلة في الماضي البسيط .

Example :

While he (to play), he (fall) down and (to break) his leg.

While he was playing, he fell down and broke his leg.

Ex. 10. **Re-write the verbs in the correct form :**

1. While I (to cross) the street, I (meet) a man with one leg.
2. He (see) me yesterday, as I (walk) along the street.

11

3. While the train (move) I (jump) out.
4. As the pupil (sleep) the teacher (come).
5. As they (to work), a man (to knock) at the door.
6. I (see) my friend as I (to drive) to the station yesterday.
7. The pupils (work) when the teacher (come) in.
8. As he (go) home last night, he (meet) Ali.
9. While that thief (escape) he (fall) down.
10. I (search) for my friend who (wait) for me near the station.
11. Last night somebody (shout) while I (study).
12. While he (sleep) in bed, a thief (break) into the house.

6. **Present Perfect** المضارع التام

١ ــ يتكون من التصريف الثالث

has أو have + Past Participle

٢ ــ تأتي has مع he أو she أو it المفرد الغائب

٣ ــ تأتي have مع باقي الضمائر

٤ ــ **يدل على حدث في الزمن الماضي ولا زال أثره موجود للوقت الحاضر**

٥ ــ نضع الفعل في الزمن المضارع التام اذا أتت احدى الكلمـات الآتية :

حديثا lately   حديثا recently   بالفعل already
توا just   منذ for   منذ since   للآن yet

Example :   The bell not yet (ring).
The bell has not yet rung.

قاعدة   Since

١ ـ اذا كان هناك فعل واحد مع Since نضع هذا الفعل في الزمن
المضارع التام. Ex. : I have lived in this house since 1950.
٢ ـ اذا اتى مع since فعـلان فنضع الفعـل الذي ياتي بعدها
مباشرة في الزمن الماضي ونضع الفعل الآخر في الزمن المضارع
التام .

I (not visit) him since he (return) from Europe.
I have not visited him since he returned from Europe.

Ex. 11 : Put the following verbs in their right form:

1. Since he (follow) my advice he (improve).
2. I just (catch) sight of the aeroplane.
3. The police officer already (permit) us to take the motor-car.
4. Since the teacher (ask) me to work, I (do) my best to succeed.
5. I (be) satisfied since he (offer) me some money.
6. Many kinds of microbes (discover) since the time of Pasteur.
7. He lately (appoint) to one of the Government offices.
8. I not (hear) of him since he (leave) for Sudan.
9. She just (draw) a nice picture.
10. The bell not yet (ring).
11. Nadia never (leave) Cairo since she (to be) two years old.
12. The thief (run) away just now.
13. I (to obey) my parents ever since I (to be) a child.
14. I (to lose) my book just now.
15. The train already (to leave) for Alexandria.

7. Past Perfect Tense الماضي التام

Had + **Past Participle** « يتكون من «التصريف الثالث

اذا أتى فعــلان في الزمن الماضي نضــع الفعل الذي حــدث اولا في
الماضي القــام (Past Perfect)
ونضع الفعــل الآخر في الماضي البسيط •

والقاعدة : before **Before,** after **After**

أي قبل كلمة **Before** وبعد كلمة **After**
نضـع الفعل في الزمن الماضي التام والفعل الآخر في الماضي البسيط •

1. He ate the cake which he had bought yesterday.
2. He had eaten the cake before he bought it yesterday.
3. He ate the cake after he had bought it yesterday.

Ex. 12 : **Correct the verbs between brackets :**

1. Ali (leave) home before his friend (come) to visit him.
2. After he (to finish) his work, he (to go) to bed.
3. Last month I (to return) to my village after I (spend) a week at Fayoum.
4. We (to write) the letter before we (to send) it.
5. After he (steal) the money he (run) away.
6. Samia (to find) the book which she (to lose) last week.
7. Shokri (eat) the food which he (buy) an hour before.
8. The train (leave) before I (to arrive).
9. Magda (tell) me that she (see) Alia yesterday.
10. The city (be) taken before help (arrive).

11. Yesterday I (beat) the dog which (bite) **my** brother.
12. The lesson (begin) after the bell (ring).
13. The man (die) before the boctor (arrive).
14. After she (write) a good composition, she (start) to study her lessons.
15. He (live) in the house which he (buy).

ملحوظات : سنتوسع في شرح الآتي في باب ال **Phrase** و ال **Clause**

١ ـ قاعدة **If**

If + present >>→ **shall** **will**
اذا أتى بعد **If** مضارع فنضع الفعل الآخر (جواب الشرط) في المستقبل

If + past >>→ should or would
اذا أتى بعد **If** **فعل ماضي فنضع مع الفعل الآخر «جواب الشرط »**
Should Would

If + Past Perfect >>→ should have or would have
اذا أتى بعد **If** فعل ماضي تام فنضع مع الفعـل الآخر (جواب الشرط)

should have, **would have.**
If it rains, I shall stay at home.
If it **rained, I should** stay at home.
If it **had rained, I should have stayed** at home.

١ ـ وعلى نفس القاعدة تكون **Unless** اذ أنها النفي لـ **if**
Unless he **works** hard, he **will fail.**
Unless he **worked** hard, he **would fail.**
Unless he **had worked** hard, he **would have failed.**

٢ ـ نضع **may** في الزمن المضارع و **might** في الزمن الماضـي بعد **in order that** و **so that** لكي
He **works** hard so that he **may** succeed.
He **worked** hard in order that he **might** succeed.

٣ ـ نضع should بعد كلمـة (lest (خشية ان)
The thief ran away **lest** the policeman **should** catch him.

Exercise 13 : Correct the verbs :

1. If the doctor permits me, I (return) to the school.
2. He sleeps early in order that he (arise) early.
3. He ran quikly lest he (miss) the train.
4. Unless we played well, we (lose) the match.
5. She studied her lessons lest the teacher (punish) her.
6. If he (make) a noise he would have been dismissed.
7. Unless he is well, he not (pay) us a visit.
8. If I had not helped him, he not (win) the prize.
9. She bought a book so that she (learn).
10. We go to the cinema in order that we (enjoy) ourselves.

Exercise 14 : Write down the past and past participle of the following verbs – اكتب تصاريف الافعال الآتية :

Tell , lead, cost, lay, teach, sweep, dream, pay, hurt, grow, bite, weave, fight, buy, spread.

GENERAL EXERCISES ON TENSES

Exercise 15 : Put the verbs in brackets in the correct tense :

1. Yesterday morning, the servant (to awake) my brother after the sun (shine) for an hour.
2. While he (play), he (fall) down and (break) his leg.

3. Our holiday not yet (begin).
4. After the policeman (go) out the thief (come) in and (steal) many valuable things.
5. I not (see) him since he (leave) for Alexandria.
6. The bell just (ring).
7. Since he (steal) the money he (frighten) of the police.
8. I (go) Port Said last week, because I (hear) that my brother (expect) to arrive from Europe where he (study) for the last five years.
9. As I (run) in the garden, I(fall) and (hurt) my arm. My father (see) me (lie) on the wet ground and he was angry because I (spoil) my clothes.
10. I (teach) at this school for four years and (to go) to secondary school next year.

Exercise 16 : Correct the verbs between brackets :

1. I have not (to lose) my book. I have (to forget) it. I (to bring) it to-morrow.
2. To-morrow, the guards (set free) the prisoner.
3. The teacher (leave) the class, after the bell (ring).
4. He always (drive) his car with great care.
5. Yesterday, I (buy) a book for my sister.

Exercise 17 : Correct the verbs between brackets :

Yesterday Ali (tear) his jacket. It (happen) in this way. While he (play) football, he (knock) another boy down. He (become) angry and they (begin) to fight. The other boy (be) older and stronger, he (seize) Ali by the collar, but Ali, in order to (escape). (twist) out of his hands (flee) away, (leap) over a wall. His jacket unfortunately (catch) on a nail and (tear).

Exercise 18 : Correct the words :

1. I (be) eleven years old, and my brother (be) older.

2. My father (go) to Cairo yesterday, and (buy) a watch.
3. I (visit) my uncle to-morrow, and he (take) me to the cinema.
4. He (get) up at six o'clock every morning and (go) to school.
5. The workman (drop) his axe into the river, while he (work).
6. Two (month) ago, he (find) the book which he (lose) in the street.
7. Ali (begin) to write his lesson yesterday but he not yet (write) it all.
8. After the man (pay) the money, I (give) him a present.
9. Yesterday the lady (feel) a pain in her ears, while she (fly) at a great (high).
10. Where you (go) yesterday ?
11. I not (see) him since last week.
12. The boy (play) tennis now.
13. Yesterday the policeman (catch) the thief while he (try) to run away.
14. The little girl (kiss) her mother before she (go) to bed last week.
15. If a thief (see) a policeman, he (run) away.

Ex. 19 : Put the verbs between brackets into the correct tense :

1. I (buy) a new coat yesterday.
2. The traveller (see) wonderful things when he (go) to Africa last year.
3. The mother (dress) her child every morning.
4. The clever boys (go) to school.
5. The River Nile (run) through Egypt and Sudan.
6. Last week my brother (go) to Alexandria and

(take) me with him.

7. The Nile (rise) in summer.
8. While I (run) across the street I fell down.
9. Since he (leave) I not (receive) any letter from him.
10. A week ago my father (buy) a new car after he (sell) the old one.
11. Unless you (answer) carefully, you (make) mistakes.
12. While we (write) the lesson, the headmaster (enter).
13. Next month, I (go) to Alex. and (swim) in the sea.
14. While he (wave) his hand, the train (start).
15. The weather (be) fine since last week.
16. The bell (ring) a few minutes ago.
17. Aly said that he (be) thankful if anybody (lend) him a book.
18. His health (improve) since he (stay) at home.
19. Why you not (to drink) the medicine yet, although you (to order) by the doctor to do so ?
20. Unless you (to work) hard last year, you (to fail).

Exercise 20 : Put the verbs between brackets in the correct form :

1. While I (walk) in Giza street yesterday, I (meet) Ali. He (say) that he (forget) his bag and he (be) afraid that the teacher (be) angry with him. This pupil usually (write) very quickly, but now he (write) slowly (hope) that he (succeed).
2. I not (see) Ali since he (come) to his town.
3. A soldier who (fight) bravely for his country (honour) by his countrymen.
4. The rich man (lie) in bed when the thief (manage) to steal his money.

5. I (give) him my pen after I (finish) writing **my** lesson.

6. Last Friday while I (study) my lessons, I (hear) someone (shout) my name in the street. I (go) **to** see who he (be). It (be) my friend Ali who (come) to visit me. He (try) to open the iron gate of **the** house. I (tell) him that if he (ring) the bell, I (go) down and (open) it for him.

   If he not (make) much noise in the class yesterday he not (punish) by the headmaster.

8. As I (walk) home last night, I (see) a blind man who (sit) on the pavement (beg) for money.

9. Last night as I (return) from the cinema I (see) a man (lie) by the roadside. He (attack) by two men who (run) away.

10. If the officer had not permitted him to return, he not (to see) his relations again.

11. Yesterday, while I (look) out of the window, I (see) a friend (walk) past. «Ali, where (go) you? Will you come and have a cup of tea with me? I (see) not you since we (leave) school four years ago» ..

12. If it (rain) next Saturday, I (be) very angry because I (agree) to go to the Nile, so that **we** (spend) a happy day (row) on the river. I not (spend) a day there since last summer, when I (save) from (drown) by a brave man after I (fall) into the water. This year I (be) more careful when I (go) lest I (fall) in again.

CONJUGATION   تصاريف الافعال

Present	المضارع	Past	الماضي	Past Participle
	يقيم	Abide	Abode	Abode
			Abided	Abided
	ينهض	Arise	Arose	Arisen
	يوقظ	Awake	Awoke	Awoke
	يحمل	Bear	Bore	Borne
	يلد	Bear	Bore	Born
	يصبح	Become	Became	Become
	يبدأ	Begin	Began	Begun
	ينظر	Behold	Beheld	Beheld
يلوي / يثني		Bend	Bent	Bent
يلتمس / يرجو		Beseech	Besought	Besought
			Beseeched	Beseeched
	يأمر	Bid	Bade	Bidden
يحزم / يضمد		Bind	Bound	Bound
	يعض	Bite	Bit	Bitten
ينزف / يدمي		Bleed	Bled	Bled
	يمزج	Blend	Blent	Blent
			Blended	Blended
	يهب	Blow	Blew	Blown
	يكسر	Break	Broke	Broken
يربي / يفرخ		Bread	Bred	Bred
	يحضر	Bring	Brought	Brought
	يذيع	Broadcast	Broadcast	Broadcast
	يبني	Build	Built	Built
	يحرق	Burn	Burnt	Burnt
	ينفجر	Burst	Burst	Burst
	يشتري	Buy	Bought	Bought
	يقدر	Can	Could	Could
	يلقي	Cast	Cast	Cast
	يمسك	Catch	Caught	Caught
	يزحف	Creep	Crept	Crept
	يختار	Choose	Chose	Chosen

Chide يؤنب	Chid	Chid
Cling يتعلق بـ	Clung	Clung
Come يأتي	Came	Come
Cost يساوي	Cost	Cost
Cut يقطع	Cut	Cut
Deal يتعامل	Dealt	Dealt
Dig يحفر	Dug	Dug
Do يعمل	Did	Done
Draw يجر / يرسم	Drew	Drown
Dream يحلم	Dreamed	Deeamed
	Dreamt	Dreamt
Drink يشرب	Drank	Drunk
Drive يقود	Drove	Driven
Dwell يقطن	Dwelt	Dwelt
	Dwelled	Dwelled
Eat ياكل	Ate	Eaten
Fall يسقط	Fell	Fallen
Feed يطعم	Fed	Fed
Feel يشعر	Felt	Felt
Fight يحارب	Fought	Fought
Fly يطير	Flew	Flown
Find يجد	Found	Found
Flee يهرب	Fled	Fled
Fling يرمي بقوة	Flung	Flung
Forbear يمتنع /يقلع	Forbore	Forbone
Forbid يمنع	Forbade	Forbidden
Forget ينسى	Forgot	Forgotten
Fortell يتنبأ	Foretold	Foretold
Forgive يعفو عن	Forgave	Forgiven
Forsake يهجر	Forsook	Forsaken
Freeze يتجمد	Froze	Frozen
Give يعطي	Gave	Given
Get يحصل على	Got	Got

يذهب	Go	Went	Gone
يطحن	Grind	Ground	Ground
ينمو / يزرع	Grow	Grew	Grown
يشنق	Hang	Hanged	Hanged
يعلق / يتعلق	Hang	Hung	Hung
يملك	Have	Had	Had
يختبىء/يخبىء	Hide	Hid	Hidden
يضرب	Hit	Hit	Hit
يسمع	Hear	Heard	Heard
يمسك	Hold	Held	Held
يحفظ / يبقي	Keep	Kept	Kept
يعزف	Know	Knew	Known
يركع	Kneel	Knelt	Knelt
يقفز	Leap	Leapt	Leapt
يتكىء	Lean	Leant	Leant
يضع	Lay	Laid	Laid
يقود	Lead	Led	Led
يتعلم	Learn	Learnt	Learnt
يرقد	Lie	Lay	Lain
يكذب	Lie	Lied	Lied
يدع / يسمح	Let	Let	Let
يترك	Leave	Left	Left
يسلف	Lend	Lent	Lent
يفقد	Lose	Lost	Lost
يضيء	Light	Lit / Lighted	Lit / Lighted
يصنع	Make	Made	Made
يمكن	May	Might	Might
يعني	Mean	Meant	Meant
يقابل	Meet	Met	Met
يقرأ	Read	Read	Read
يستأجر	Rend	Rent	Rent
يركب	Ride	Rode	Ridden

ينهض / يطلع	Rise	Rose	Risen
يدق / يدوي	Ring	Rang	Rung
يجري	Run	Ran	Run
يقول	Say	Said	Said
يرى	See	Saw	Seen
يبحث عن	Seek	Sought	Sought
يبيع	Sell	Sold	Sold
يرسل	Send	Sent	Sent
يغرب	Set	Set	Set
يحيك يخيط	Sew	Sewed	Sown
يهز	Shake	Shook	Shaken
سوف	Shall	Should	Should
يضيء	Shine	Shone	Shone
ينتعل الحذاء	Shoe	Shod	Shod
يرمي بالرصاص	Shoot	Shot	Shot
يرى – يعرض	Show	Showed	Shown
ينكمش	Shrink	Shrank	Shrank
يذبح	Slay	Slew	Slain
ينام	Sleep	Slept	Slept
ينزلق – يتزحلق	Slide	Slid	Slid
يقذف	Sling	Slung	Slung
ينسل خلسة	Slink	Slunk	Slunk
يشق	Slit	Slit	Slit
يغني	Sing	Sang	Sung
يغرق – يغوص	Sink	Sunk	Sunk
يجلس	Sit	Sat	Sat
يشم	Smell	Smelt	Smelt
يضرب	Smite	Smote	Smitten
يبذر	Sow	Sowed	Sown
يتكلم	Speak	Spoke	Spoken
يتهجى	Spell	Spelt	Spelt
ينفق	Spend	Spent	Spent
يسكب	Spill	Spilt	Spilt
		Spilled	Spilled

يسرع	Speed	Speeded / Sped	Speeded / Sped
يغزل	Spin	Spun	Spun
يبصق	Spit	Spat	Spat
يشق	Split	Split	Split
يتلف	Spoil	Spoilt	Spoilt
ينشر	Spread	Spread	Spread
يقفـز	Spring	Sprang	Sprung
يقف	Stand	Stood	Stood
يسرق	Steal	Stole	Stolen
يلصق	Stick	Stuck	Stuck
يلدغ	Sting	Stung	Stung
تنبعث منه رائحة	Stink	Stank	Stunk
يوسع الخطى	Stride	Strode	Stridden
ينظم في خيط	String	Strung	Strung
يدق ، يصك	Strike	Struck	Struck
يناضل	Strive	Strove	Striven
يقسم (يحلف)	Swear	Swore	Sworn
يكنس	Sweep	Swept	Swept
ينتفخ ـ يتضخم	Sweel	Swelled	Swollen
يسبح ـ يعوم	Swim	Swam	Swum
يتمايل	Swing	Swung	Swung
يأخذ	Take	Took	Taken
يعلم	Teach	Taught	Taught
يمزق	Tear	Tore	Torn
يخبر	Tell	Told	Told
يظن	Think	Thought	Thought
يزدهر	Thrive	Throve	Thriven
يرمي	Throw	Threw	Thrown
يقذف	Thrust	Thrust	Thrust
يدوس ـ يطأ	Tread	Trod	Trodden
يوقظ / يستيقظ	Wake	Woke	Woke
يرتدي	Wear	Wore	Worn

ينسج Weave	Wove	Woven
يبكي Weep	Wept	Wept
سوف Will	Would	
يكسب Win	Won	Won
يلف Wind	Wound	Wound
يعصر الملابس Wring	Wrung	Wrung
يكتب Write	Wrote	Written

PASSIVE AND ACTIVE VOICE
المبني للمعلوم والمبني للمجهول

للتغيير من مبني للمعلوم Active الى مبني للمجهول Passive نتبع الخطوات الآتية : ـ

١ ـ المفعول به يصير فاعلا (يعرف المفعول به بوجوده بعد الفعل مباشرة)

٢ ـ نضع فعل to be في نفس زمن الجملة ٠٠

٣ ـ نضع الفعل الاصلي في التصريف الثالث ٠

٤ ـ نضع الفاعل مسبوقا بكلمة By

Examples:-

1. He writes the lesson.
    The lesson **is written** by him.
2. He wrote the lesson.
    The lesson **was written** by him.
3. She **will write** the lesson.
    The lesson **will be written** by her.
4   Ali is **writing** the lesson.
    The lesson **is being written** by Ali.
5. Fatma has written the lesson.
    The lesson **has been written** by Fatma.

(1) Verb to be: am, is, are, was, were.   ملحوظة :

٢ ـ كل فعل مساعد نضع معه   **be**

٣ ـ has, have, had تأخذ   **been**

PRONOUNS   الضمائر

SUBJECT ضمائر الفاعل		OBJECT ضمائر المفعول به
I	أنا	me
he	هو	him
she	هي	her
you	أنت ـ أنتم	you
they	هم	them
we	نحن	us
it	لغير العاقل	it

Exersise 21. Change into the passive voice:-
1. The old woman gave the Prince nice food.
2. We **shall conquer** them.
3. The thief **has stolen** the money.
4. Some people **eat meat** for breakfast.
5. He **played** football well.
6. The girl **lost** her watch.
7. I **eat** a cake every day.
8. He **has written** some words.
9. She **was buying** a book.
10. I **teach** my brother English.

Exercise 22. Rewrite beginning with the black-type words:-
1. He bought **some eggs** from the farmer.
2. Sometimes a great battle is won by **a small army**.
3. He killed **a bear.**
4. He gave the boy **a present.**
5. The miller grinds **corn** into flour.
6. The stone-cutters were cutting **an obelisk** of a great mass of rock.
7. He has always **obeyed my orders.**
8. The last war left **many towns** in ruins.
9. His trick deceived **me.**
10. The teachers read **the lessons.**

Exercise 23: Change into Passive voice:
1. She cooks food.
2. I visited my friend.
3. We shall play football.
4. They are answering questions.
5. He has eaten fruit.
6. The aeroplanes dropped many bombs on the town.
7. We can not reach the ceiling.
8. Dirt causes illness.

9. The doctor is examining the child.
10. The learned men ·discovered how to read the ancient writings.
11. A strong army will conquer the enemy.
12. The carpenter knocked some nails into the chair.
13. A tidy boy arranges his books nicely in his desk.
14. The wind drives sailing ships over the water.
15. The policeman caught the thief although he ran fast.

ACTIVE & PASSIVE   المبني للمعلوم والمبني للمجهول

B. QUESTION

للتغيير الى المبني للمجهول في السؤال اتبـــع نفس الخطوات السابقة ثم ضع الفعل قبل الفاعل واذا كان هنـــاك حرف استفهام فضعه في الاول

1. Does he write the lesson?
The lesson **is written** by him. **Is** the lesson written by him?
2. Did I write the lesson?
The lesson **was written** by me. **Was** the lesson written by me?
3. Will Ali write the lesson?
The lesson **will be written** by Ali. **Will** the lesson be written by Ali?
4. **Why** is Sami **writing** the lesson?
The lesson **is being written** by Sami. **Why is** the lesson being written by Sami?
5. **Who** wrote the lesson?
The lesson was written **by whom. By whom** was the lesson written?
6. Who was seen by you? **Whom** did you see?
Whom did you see?

C. COMMAND ‏الامر

‏لتغيير الامر من مبني للمعلوم الى مبني للمجهول اتبع الخطوات
‏الآتية :

‏١ ـ المفعول به يعتبر فاعلا
‏٢ ـ ضع فعل to be في نفس الزمن اي الامر فيكون be
‏٣ ـ ضع التصريف الاصلي في التصريف الثالث
‏٤ ـ ضع كلمة Let في اول الجملة

1. **Write** the lesson.
   The lesson **be written**. Let the lesson be written.
2. **Open** the door.
   The door **be opened**. Let the door be opened.

Exercise 24: Change into passive voice:-

1. Can you see germs?
2. Who told you this story?
3. Have you heard the story of the prisoner?
4. Do you often meet these boys?
5. Who broke the window?
6. Shut the book.
7. Does the gardner water the flowers?
8. Read the lesson.
9. Has anybody seen my fountain-pen?
10. Who has borrowed the books?

Exercise 25. Change into Passive:-

1. Nadia **takes** care of her books.
2. She **has dressed** her baby.
3. The teacher **explained** the lesson.
4. Zaki **will buy** a house.
5. We **must** study our lessons.
6. He **may** write a letter.
7. Nagi **is making** a noise.
8. The dog **was guarding** the hut.

9. Hoda **had killed** the bird.
10. Who drank the milk?
11. Why shall we kill flies?
12. When will you visit me?
13. Who broke the window?
14. Whom did they visit?
15. Who wrote the exercise?

Exercise 26 : Rewrite the following sentences beginning with the words in brackets:

a) The camel was carrying **(a heavy load)** .
b) She has given her sisters **(many presents).**
c) I shall wind **(a string)** round my finger.
d) Because he was angry, he said **(some insulting words).**
e) He left **(the university)** although he was clever.

Exercise 27. Change into passive voice:

1. She has asked me two questions.
2. The boys have seen their father.
3. I'll show you the market.
5. The teacher has punished the lazy boys.
4 He did not eat the two apples.
6. He has told them a nice story.
7. Farmers in Egypt grow cotton, wheat and maize.
8. The army could not defend the city.
9. A merchant buys a car for L.E. 500.
10. The donkey is pulling the cart along the street.
11. He has sold all his possessions.
12. Did the servant ring the bell?
13. Write a letter to your father.
14. He had taken strong drink.
15. Were the men cutting down the tree?

PASSIVE & ACTIVE المبني للمجهول والمبني للمعلوم

للتغيير من مبني للمجهول (Passive) الى مبني للمعلوم
(Active)   اتبع الخطوات الآتية : ـ
١ ـ احذف By وهات ما بعدها فاعلا في اول الجملة
٢ ـ احذف فعل To Be وهات الفعل الاصلي في نفس زمن فعـل
To Be
٣ ـ ضع الفاعل في آخر الجملـة اي يرجع مفعولا به مثال :

1. The lesson is written **by** Ali. Ali **writes** the lesson.
2. The lesson **was** written **by** her. She **wrote** the lesson.
3. The lesson will be written **by** them.
   They will **write** the lesson.
4. The lesson has **been** written **by** him.
   He has **written** the lesson.
5. The lesson is **being** written **by** Mary.
   Mary is **writing** the lesson.
6. By whom was the lesson written? Who wrote the lesson?
7. **Let** the lesson **be** written. write the lesson.

Exercise 28. Change into active voice:-
1. The thief is caught by the policeman.
2. The child was run over by a motor-car.
3. By whom was the mirror broken?
4. Are the flowers watered by the gardener?
5. The workmen are not being paid by their employer.
6. A letter can be written by her.
7. The book has been found by Ali.
8. By whom was he beaten?
9. The cat **is beaten** by the boy.
10. The bell **was being rung** by him.
11. **Bread is being sold** by them.

12. The food will be eaten by the baby.
13. The mice are caught by the cat.
14. The branches were shaken by the wind.

NEGATION النفي

في النفي نضع كلمة not بعد الفعل المساعد
والأفعال المساعدة هي :

(1) have, has, had.
(2) **Verb to be:** am, is, are, was.
(3) shall, will, should, would.
(4) may, might, must, ought to.
(5) can, could.

واذا لم يكن هناك فعل مساعد فنأتي بفعل مساعد ·

أ ــ فاذا كان الفعل مضارعا وآخره «S» فاننا عند النفي نضع
does not قبل الفعل ونحذف حرف «S» من الفعل مثال :
He writes a lesson. He does not write a lesson.

ب ــ واذا كان الفعل مضارعا ليس آخره «S» فنضع قبل الفعل
«do not» مثل :
We play football. We do not play football.

جـ ــ اذا كان الفعل ماضيا فاننا عند نفي الجملة نضع **«did not»**
قبل الفعل ونحول الفعل الى مصدر (مضارع) مثل :
I visited him.   I did not visit him.

Exercise 29. Change into negative:-
1. They played in the class.
2. She cooks food.
3. The baby drinks milk.
4. We shall go to the cinema.
5. You pay attention.
6. She can sweep the floor.
7. The dog guards the field.
8. They come to school early.
9. He is running in the garden.
10. You bought a book yesterday.

د ــ واذا كانت هناك احدى الكلمات الآتية في الجملة فتنفى الجملة
بتغيير الكلمة بما يقابلها في الجدول الآتي فقط : ــ

AFFIRMATIVE اثبات	NEGATIVE نفي
some بعض every كل	no not ...... any
and Both ...... and كلا الاثنين either ...... or هذا او ذلك	neither ...... nor لا هذا ٠٠ ولا ذاك
always دائما often غالبا sometimes احيانا	never أبدا
All كل	not all
and so وأيضا	not ...... neither
also أيضا	not ...... either
as ...... as مثل	not so ...... as
I saw some birds.	I saw no birds I did not see any bird.
He-reads **and** writes English well **Either** Ahmed or Ali broke the glass. **Both** you **and** he are absent	He **neither reads nor** writes English well. **Neither** Ahmed **nor** Ali broke the glass. **Neither** you **nor** he is absent.
He **sometimes** drives his car.	He **never** drives his car.
All the pupils passed.	Not **all** the pupils passed.
I went to the cinema **and so did** my brother.	I did **not** go to the cinema neither did my brother.
I bought a pair of shoes also.	I did not buy a pair of shoes either.

He is as clever as his brother.	He is not so clever as his brother.

Exercise 30. Change into negative:-

1. You have seen this picture **also.**
2. My brother **sometimes** helps me.
3. Every boy received a prize.
4. He runs **as** quickly **as** his brother.
5. The servant lost ten piastres yesterday, and so did I.
6. He **always** wastes his time.
7. I met **both** Ali **and** Ahmed.
8. **Somebody** is waiting for us.
9. **All** the servants are honest.
10. He forgot either his book **or** his pen.

Exercise 31. Change into negative:-

1. I have been in Alexandria also.
2. You can obtain some money in this way.
3. Somebody is playing in the garden.
4. On the moon, there is water also.
5. This man is either a robber or a beggar.
6. **Everyone** of them can sing.
7. He ought to do so.
8. Animals know all these things.
9. He always writes with a pencil.

10. Both he and his friend are in France.

11. There are germs everywhere.

12. They sometimes visit us.

13. He always comes late.

14. He always eats much fruit.

15. All the pupils were at school.

16. Hassan has a car also.

17. He did his work too.

18. I shall tell everybody what you are doing.

19. He will have either the book or the pen.

20. I bought some books.

HOW TO ASK QUESTIONS?

اذا كان السؤال عن كلمة في اول الجملة (فاعل) نسأل بكلمة
Who اذا كان السؤال عن العاقل ، او بكلمة What اذا كان السؤال
عن غير العاقل ونضع باقي الجملة بدون تغيير ٠

The boy comes to school. **Who** comes to school ?
The birds sing on the tree. **What** sing on the tree ?

اذا كان السؤال عن كلمة ليست في اول الجملة نبحث عن نوعهــا
حسب حروف الاستفهام ونضع بعده فعلا مساعدا فاذا لم يكن هناك
فعل مساعد في الجملة نضع did اذا كان الفعل ماضيا ، does
اذا كان الفعل مضارعا فيه حرف«S» ، do اذا كان الفعل مضارعا
بدون حرف «S»

Who	للفاعل العاقل	Whom	للمفعول به العاقل
What	لغير العاقل	Why	لماذا (للسبب)
When	متى (للزمان)	Where	اين (الامكان)
How	كيف (للحال)	How many	كم (للعدد)
Whose	لمن (للملكية)	How old	كم (للعمر)

Examples

I met **my friend**.

    Whom did I meet ?

He goes **to school** every day.

    Where does he go every day ?

We come **at 8 o'clock**.

    When do we come ?

We come to school **to learn**.

    Why do we come to school?

I saw **Ali's** father.

    Whose father did I see ?

Exercise 32. Ask questions to the words in black type:
1. **The woodman** killed a bear.

2. **Ali and Sami** have books.
3. **She** saw a bird.
4. The **clever boys** go to school.
5. **The cat** ran after the mice.
6. **The cow** gives us milk.
7. **The Nile** rises in summer.
8. The **magic looking-glass** could answer questions.
9. She saw **her brother** in the street.
10. The King married a **beautiful woman.**
11. He will meet **Ali** to-morrow.
12. The boy thanks **him.**
13. He saw a **cow.**
14. The man has a hat.
15. He shot a **bear.**
16. Ali drinks **some water.**
17. He put his handkerchief **in his pocket.**
18. We were looking **at the blackboard.**
19. The dwarfs stayed **by the box.**
20. We went to **his friend's house.**
21. This is **Ali's** house.
22. **The soldier's** leg was broken.
23. **The boy's** bag was lost.
24. I met **your brother.**
25. He went home **because he was tired.**
26. A horse goes to the river **because it wants to drink.**
27. We come to school **to learn.**
28. The child was weeping because **his mother went out.**
29. He will come **to-morrow.**
30. They get up **in the morning.**

38

31. He goes to the cinema **once a week.**
32. They come to school **at seven o'clock.**

استعمالات   **How**

١ ــ تستعمل   **How**   للسؤال عن الحالة او الكيفية مثل :
He was **very pleased** to meet his friend.
How was he to meet his friend ?

٢ ــ تستعمل **How many** للسؤال عن العدد مثل :
Thirty boys are in this class.
How many boys are in this class ?

٣ ــ تستعمل   **How much**   للسؤال عن الكمية مثل :
You paid **five pounds** for this coat.
How much did you pay for this coat ?

٤ ــ تستعمل   **How old**   للسؤال   عن العمر مثل : ــ
I am **twenty years old.**   **How old** are you ?

٥ ــ تستعمل   **How far**   للسؤال عن المسافات مثل : ــ
It is **240 kilometers** from Cairo to Alexandria.
How far is it from Cairo to Alexandria ?

٦ ــ تستعمل   **How long**   للسؤال عن الاطوال مثل : ــ
This rope is **two meters** long.
How long is this rope ?

٧ ــ تستعمل   **How high**   للسؤال عن الارتفاعات مثل : ــ
This fence is **four meters** high.
How high is this fence ?

٨ ــ تستعمل   **How tall**   للسؤال عن اطوال الاشخاص مثل : ــ
Sami is a **meter and a half.**   **How tall** is Sami ?

Exercise 33.   Ask questions :
1. The old man walked **slowly.**
2. He shot the rabbit **with a gun.**
3. She looked **very tired.**

4. He goes to school **by train.**
5. Zaki is 165cm **tall.**
6. It is **seven miles** from Cairo to the Pyramids.
7. A bus carries **thirty** passengers.
8. You will pay **ten piasters** for this book.
9. People can travel from Cairo to Alex. **by aeroplane.**
10. This wall **is two feet high.**
11. I have **two** hands.
12. The room has **three** windows.
13. There are **forty** boys in the class-room.
14. He is **twelve years** old.

**Exercise 34.   Fill in the spaces with a suitable interro-
    gative word :**

ضع حرف الاستفهام المناسب في المكان الخالي :

1. .... do you live ? . 2 ...... fingers have you ?
3...... did you lend your book ? 4. ...... visited you?
5. From ...... do tourists come ? 6. ...... is it from
Caïro to Tanta ? 7. ...... will he go to the cinema ?
8. ...... did she lose yesterday ? 9. From ...... bag
did you take the pencil ? 10 .... is the pyramid?

ملحوظة : وقد يعطيك الممتحن الاجابة فقط ويطلب منك تكويـن
السؤال ، وفي هذه الحالة تضع الكلمة (المراد الاستفهام عنها)
في جملة ثم تكون سؤالا • مثال :

1. **In the class.** The boy is **in the class. Where** is the
    boy ?
2. **Interesting.** The story is **interesting. How** is the
    story ?

Exercise 35. Write questions for the following answers:
1. Regularly.
2. In Central Africa.

2. Houses are built of stone.
4. Next door to the school.
5. In summer.
6. Forty piastres.
7. Seven miles.
8. Fifty pupils.
9. Quickly.
10. Because he was late.
11. Twenty five piastres.
12. The bell rings **at 8 o'clock.**
13. For his honesty.
14. Because it is hot.
51. At the theatre.
16. I should send a telegram.
17. He comes to school **on foot.**
18. Because the road was blocked.
19. Because he was ill.
20. The aeroplane can travel **400 miles an hour.**
21. The band stopped playing at **ten o'clock.**
22. On the Mokattam hills.
23. There are **12 months** in a year.
24. No, sir, my father is not at home.
25. They will visit us **next Friday.**

DIRECT & INDIRECT SPEECH الكلام المباشر وغير المباشر

(1)	Statement. جملة اخبارية	(2)	Question. سؤال
(3)	Command. طلب	(4)	Exclamation. تعجب

الجملة الاخبارية   STATEMENT - 1

للتغيير من الكلام المباشر الى غير المباشر تتبع الخطوات الآتية:

١ ـ احذف الاقواس المفتوحة وضـع كلمة «That»

٢ ـ غير الضمائر حسب المعنى

٣ ـ غير بعض الافعال والكلمات حسب الجدول الآتي :

Direct	الكلام المباشر	Indirect الكلام غير المباشر
Now	الآن	then
this	هذا	that
these	هؤلاء	those
here	هنا	there
to-day	اليوم	that day
to-morrow	غدا	the next day, the following day
yesterday	امس	the day before, the previous day
ago	منذ	before
thus	هكذا	so
said to	قال	told
present tense	المضارع	past tense
Past Tense	الماضي	Past Perfect

Example :

(1) He said to me, «I shall see you to-morrow.»
He told me that he would see me the next day.

(2) Ali said, «I went to the cinema yesterday.»

Ali said that he had gone to the cinema the day before.

ملحوظة : اذا كان هناك « · » بين جملتين لشخص متكلم واحد
فضع بدلا منها and that او and added that

I said to him. «I shall see you to-morrow. We shall visit Ali.»

I told him that I should see him the next day and that we should visit Ali.

٢ ــ اذا كانت كلمة said في اخر الجملة فضعها في اول الجملة
لتضع بعدها حرف الوصل that مثال : ــ

1. «I wrote my lesson yesterday.», the boy said.
    The boy said that he had written his lesson the day before.

٣ ــ اذا كانت كلمة القول (say) في المضارع حينئذ لا تغير ازمنة
الجملة وانما التغيير يكون فقط في الضمائر والكلمــات حسب
الجدول مثال : ــ

1. She says, «I shall cook the food to-morrow.»
    She says that she will cook the food the next day.
2. We say, «We are playing football now.»
    We say that we are playing football then.

Exercise 36. Change into indirect speech :

1. At last he said, «I cannot go on any more. I have never been so hungry in my life.»
2. The teacher always says, «This is the worst class I have met till now.»
3. The teacher said, «This boy was absent during the accident. I hope that everything will be clear by to-morrow.»
4. They said : «We have found this coat». «It is my son's coat.» Jacob said.
5. He said, «I have no money with me now, but I shall give you some money to-morrow.»

6. Everyone shouted, «He is drowning and cannot swim.»
7. He said, «I cannot return to-day or to-morrow».
8. The man says «I am a guilty man, and deserve punishment.»
9. I said to Ali: «You can go to-morrow.»
10. The criminal said : «I am going to confess. I robbed the man of his money, and gave it to my brother.»
11. Amina has said to her mother : «I am mistaken. I shall not do this another time.»
12. The lady said: «I cannot pay this high price.»
13. «I am going away a week from to-day.», said the man.
14. The boy said : «I have found this book». «It is my book.», said Ali.
15. «You promised to tell me a story.», said the boy to his father.

How to change from Indirect to Direct :

للتغيير من كلام غير مباشر Indirect الى كلام مباشر Direct اتبع الآتي : ـ

١ ـ told تصبح said to

٢ ـ احذف كلمة that وضع بدلا منها فاصلة واقواسا مفتوحة .

٣ ـ رجع الكلمات والافعال الى اصلهـــا ، اي ان المـــاضي يصبح مضارعا والماضي التام يصير ماضيا بسيطا .

٤ ـ غير الضمائر الى صيغة المتكلم او المخاطب .

٥ ـ لا تنس وضع الاقواس المفتوحة في آخر الجملة .

Example :

1. The servant told his master that he could not return that day or the next day.

   The servant said to his master : «I cannot return to-day or to-morrow.»

2. She said that she had cooked nice food the day before.

She said: «I cooked nice food yesterday.»

Exercise 37 : Change into Direct Speech :

a) He said that he would come as soon as he could.

b) The station-master told me that the train had gone and that there was not another train until the next day.

c) He told me that I might leave that place as soon as I could.

d) Ali stated that he would have been top of the class, if he had not been prevented by illness from attending school then.

e) He wrote to me saying that he would expect me to arrive the following Friday.

f) She said that she had never seen so many beautiful flowers.

g) The boy said that he would go for a ride on his bicycle.

h) Patruchio told her father that he loved her more than ever and that he had prepared everything for their marriage the following day.

i) The officer thought that the knight could meat the bravest of their warriors.

j) The boy told his father that he had succeeded and that he wanted a bicycle as a reward.

k) He said that he felt sure that there was some fearful quarrel in the room.

l) They said that they had not heard of a more exciting event before.

m) He said that he was not interested in other people's matters.

n) They promised us to pay the money the next day.

2. QUESTION السؤال

لتغيير السؤال من كلام مباشر الى غير مباشر اتبع الخطوات الآتية : ـ

١ ـ said او said to تصبح asked

٢ ـ احذف الاقواس المفتوحة وضـع كلمة if او whether اذا لم يكن هناك حرف استفهام .

٣ ـ يبقى حرف الاستفهام اذا كان هناك .

٤ ـ ضع الفاعل قبل الفعل (اي غير الى النوع المثبت)

٥ ـ غير الكلمات والافعال حسب الجدول السابق

1. The teacher said to the pupil : «Where are you going now?».
   The teacher asked the pupil where he was going then.

2. I said to the gardener : «Are the apples ripe?».
   I asked the gardener if the apples were ripe.

Exercise 38 : Change into Indirect speech :

1. I said to Ali : «To whom did you give my book last night?».

2. He says to the policeman : «Which way leads to the station?».

3. He said to me : «What time is it? Are you coming now?».

4. I shall say to Nabil : «Are you sure he will come?».

5. I said to my brother : «Don't you remember that when you went away you took your book away?».

6. «**Would** you like to take this drug?» said the doctor to the sick man.

7. I said to him, «**Were** you absent yesterday?»

8. «What is your name?» said the teacher to the new pupil, «and how old are you?»

9. «Will you not stay with me for one night and be

my messenger?» said the soldier to the swallow.
«The boy may die of thirst, and the mother may
die of grief.»

10. «Who was absent yesterday?»the headmaster said.

11. «Can you lend me a piastre?» whispered my
brother.

12. I said to my servant, «Have my shoes been cleaned?».

13. «What do you want now?» said the father to his
son.

14. He exclaimed in anger. «Why are you so late and
where have you been?»

15. The tailor said to me, «Do you want a woollen
suit?»

16. «Who was here yesterday?», the teacher said.

17. My mother said to the servant, «Did you break
these plates?».

18. I said to the butcher's son, «Waht are you doing
with this knife? Do you want to kill us?»

19. Ali said to me, «Will you go to Alex this summer?»

20. The policeman said to the driver, «What is the number of your car? Why do you drive so fast?».

**How to change from indirect to direct speech in
question :**

للتغيير من كلام غير مباشر indirect الى كلام مباشر direct
في السؤال اتبع الخطوات الآتية :

١ ـ asked تصبح said او said to اذا كان هناك
مخاطب مثال : I said to my son: ﴾ ﴿ I asked my son

٢ ـ اذا وجدنا كلمة if او whether فنفهم من ذلك عدم وجود
حرف استفهام مما يستلزم وضع فعل مساعد كحرف استفهام ووضع
اقواس مفتوحة قبلها .

I asked my son if he drank the milk.
I said to my son, «Do you drink the milk?»

٣ ــ ضع الفعل قبل الفاعل ثم غيــر الافعــال فاذا كان الفعل ماضيا
Past يصبــح مضارعـــا Present واذا كان ماضيا تاما
Present Perfect يصبح اما مضارعا تاما Past Perfect
او مـــــاضيا Past . ثم غير الكلمات حسب الجدول
السابق وضع علامة استفهـــــــام واقفل الاقواس المفتوحة .
٤ ــ وعادة تغير الضمائر التي بين الاقواس الى المتكلم او المخاطب

I asked the pupil if he **had written** his exercise.
I said to the pupil, «**Have you written** your exercise?»
I said to the pupil, «**Did you write** your exercise?»

Exercise 39. Change into Direct Speech:

1. I asked Ali if it was necessary to dip a fountain pen in the ink.

2. I asked the gardner what he knew about the old man and who he was.

3 . Mohammed asked his sister whether she did **not** think that was a good idea.

4. The sick man asked the doctor whether it was necessary for him to keep in bed all the time.

5. My father asked me if I had done my home-work for the following day, and if my teachers were satisfied with me.

6. He asked me about my age and my address.

7. The judge asked him by whom he had been robbed and how much he had lost.

8. I asked him who had helped him, when he had arrived and where he was going the next day.

9. The boy told his father that he had succeeded and asked when he would buy him the watch.

10. The Boy Scout told the tourist that he would take him to wherever he wished to go, as he was free

that morning. The tourist replied that he was very kind, but that if he could direct him to the station all would be well, as he had a train to catch in ten minutes from then.

---

3. COMMAND   الامر

للتغيير من كلام مباشر الى غير مباشر في الامر اتبع الخطوات الآتية :

اولا :

١ – said تصبح **ordered** اذا كان الكلام من شخص اكبر الى شخص اصغر

٢ – said تصبح **begged** او **prayed** اذا كان الكلام مـــن شخص اصغر الى اكبر وخاصة اذا كانت هناك كلمة **please**

٣ – said تصبح **told** اذا كان الشخصان متساويان .

٤ – s̲a̲i̲d̲ تصبح **advised** اذا كانت هناك نصيحة .

ثانيا : احذف الاقواس المفتوحة وضع كلمة «**to**» قبل الفعل .

ثالثا : احذف كلمتي **Please, do** من الجملة .

رابعا : غير بعض الكلمات حسب الجدول السابق .

Example:-

1. I said to the servant, «Bring me a glass of water.»
    I ordered the servant to bring me a glass of water.
2. The son said to his father, «Please, forgive me this time.»
    The son begged his father to forgive him that time.
3. He said to me, «Do not do this again.»
    He told me not to do that again.

Exercise 40. Change into indirect speech:

1. He said to me, «Please lend me some money.»
2. «Write your name clearly», said the teacher to the pupil.
3. The master said to the servant, «Go at once and bring me a pen with which I can write».

4. Ali said to Zaki, «Let me ride your bicycle for half an hour.»

5. The judge said to the policeman, «Take him back to prison. Do not let him escape again.»

6. «Do not leave me alone.», the child said.

7. The beggar said to me, «Please give me a piastre. I am weak.»

8 The prisoner said to the judge, «I am innocent. Please take pity on my poor childern.»

9. Ali said to him, «Please look for him because my father is here.»

10. I said to my father, «Please, excuse the mistake I made.»

11. Fahmi said, «Come to my house and see me this afternoon, Ali.»

12. The father said to his son, «Leave me alone and tell your mother that I am busy.»

13. «Please give me some water», said the wounded man to me. «I'm dying of thirst.»

14. The doctor said to my friend. «You are ill. Go home and go to bed. I will come to see you to-morrow.»

15. He said to his guest, «Please stay for the party.»

16. «Work hard Ali», said his father «I shall give you five pounds if you pass your examination.»

17. The officer said to him, «Tell me your name or I shall send you to prison.»

18. The policeman said to him, «Stop. You can't go on any further.»

19. «Do not play with this thing when I am speaking to you.», he said to his son.

20. Ahmed said to Mohamed, «Don't leave me now. Why do you want to go when you have been here for only a minute?».

4. EXCLAMATION   التعجب

لتغيير التعجب من كلام مباشر الى كلام غير مباشر اتبــــع الخطوات الآتية :

١ ـ احذف كلمة التعجب وضع بدلا منها كلمة تدل عليها مثل :

with regret بندم   with anger بغضب   with joy بفرح
with sorrow بأسف

٢ ـ احذف الاقواس المفتوحة وضع كلمة that

٣ ـ غير الضمائر والافعال حسب النوع الاول (الجملة الاخبارية)

ملحوظة : كلمات التعجب ، اما **حرف استفهام استعمل ككلمـــة تعجب مثل** what, how وتعرفها بوجود علامة تعجب في نهاية الجملة ، او كلمة تعجب بذاتها مثل (**Alas** يا للاسف) (**Hurrah** مرحبا) (**Oh** يـــا) وتعرفها بوجود عــلامة التعجب بعدها مباشرة ·

1. He said, «Alas! I shall not recover my fortune.»
   He said with sorrow that he would not recover his fortune.

2. He said, «How foolish I have been!»
   He said with regret that he had been foolish.

Exercise 41. Change into indirect speech:-

1. The pupils shouted, «Hurrah! Our team has won the match.»
2. The porter said, «How heavy this bag is!»
3. The father said, «Alas! There is no hope in his recovery.»
4. He said to me, «How beautiful your garden is!».
5. The pupil cried, «Hurrah! I have passed my examination.»
6. He shouted, «What a mistake I have made.»
7. The beggar said, «Alas! I am dying of hunger.»
8. The Egyptians said, «Hurrah! We have defeated

the Britsh, French and Israeli armies in Port-Said.»

9. The Egyptian pilot said, «Hurrah! I have destroyed the enemy's harbour.»

10. I said to my friend, «How fine your clothes are!».

GENERAL EXERCISES

Exercise 42. Turn into the indirect speech:-

1. He said to me, «I shall visit you to-morrow.»

2. He said to the policeman, «Did you catch the thief yesterday?».

3. The man said to owner of the house, «I shall rent this flat. How much will you charge me?».

4. The little girl said to her mother, «Where can I find my book, mother?» «I do not know.», answered the mother. «Look for it in your room because I saw it there yesterday».

5. Ali said to Hassan, «Have you seen my brother to-day?».

6. Hassan said, «I saw him yesterday.»

7. «I think that he may come soon», said I to my brother.

8. Ali said, «Thank you very much.»

9. Petruchio said to himself, «I'll tame her and teach her to obey. I can see an improvement already.»

10. Pyecraft said to me, «I've tried Western drugs. Can you give me bit of your grandmother's stuff? It may reduce my weight.»

11. «This is your room.», said the father to his son.

12. Samy said, «I shall fly to Italy to-morrow.»

13. Tom is saying to me, «Are you ill?».

14. «Do you like to be with us?», said his friend. «We are going to visit the market.»

15. «Why **did** you not go to your uncle as I told you?», said the father to the boy. «You deserve a severe beating; **go** now and bring the books in this bag.»
16. The doctor said to me, «How did you break your arm?».
17. «May I go home now?», said the boy to the teacher. «I have finished all I have got to do to-day.»
18. «Put your books in your desks,» said the teacher, «but do not be late to-morrow as you will have an examination.»
19. He said to Ali, «Are you coming here tomorrow to talk about this matter?».
20. My father often says to me, «Are you working hard?».
21. Tom said to me, «Were you ill yesterday?».
22. The man said to me «I have not a job for two months and I have a wife and family to keep. Can you give me some work ? I am a carpenter». I replied, «I have nothing to give you to-day but if you can come to-morrow, I shall find you some.» He said, «Thank you; I shall certainly be here to-morrow morning.»
23 He said, «I feel ill. May I go home ? I can not do any work.»
24. Mr. Smith said to the applicant, «How fast can you type?» The applicant replied, «I can type eight words a minute». Mr. Smith said, «Let me see your letters of recommendation. I want the copies only and you may keep the originals».
25. The servant said, «I shall send the letter at once».

Exercise 43. Change into indirect:-

1. He said to the boys, «We shall hardly reach the falls tonight at this rate. Make haste and do not

waste your time».

2. He said to his friend. «I shall come here to-morrow».

3. He said, «Come along up on deck, boys. I shall keep you under guard».

4. The doctor said to the girl, «Why did you not come to see me yesterday? You are very feverish now».

5. «Why were you late yesterday? Can you never come early? If you are late to-morrow you will be dismissed .», said the headmaster to the boy.

6. «Don't drive too fast, Ali.», Sami told him, «We are not in a great hurry».

7. «What are you doing here?» a foreign voice asked.

8 Ali said to his friend, «Good morning, where are you going now? I want to go with you to the cinema».

9. His father said, « If he goes abroad, he will be the most miserable boy that ever was born. I can give no consent to it».

10. «I am glad to meet you both». I said to the pupils.

11. «Do you think he is quite honest?» Ali asked.

12. I said to Ali, «Please, go and call a doctor now».

13. The boy said to his father, «Please take me to the circus».

14. The friend **has** often said, «When are you coming to see me?».

15. The teacher said to his puils, «Have you been to the zoo?».

16. «Will you confess that you are guilty?», said the judge. «I shall not, as **I** am not guilty.», answered the prisoner. «Do you know the criminal?», asked the judge. «You may ask the police, sir», replied the prisoner.

17. He said to me, «Do you like eating the meat of pigs? A man who eats that kind of meat will look like a pig».

18. The shopkeeper said, «I have no fruit to-day. Can I offer you anything else? My tinned fruit is very fresh».

19. The merchant said to the builder, «Build me a house like that of a prince. Do not forget to surround it with a garden. In six months I hope to occupy it».

20. The traveller said to the guide, «Is there anyone here who speaks French ? I do not know any other language».

21. «Why do the Japanese build their houses of paper?», said **the small boy**. «There are earthquakes in Japan», **said his father**. «When the houses fall down, what do they do?», **said the small boy**. «They carry them off to another place», **said his father.**

22. When we had finished, he said: «There will be no more work until to-morrow. Bring your tools with you and be ready to start at seven o'clock».

23. «I have heard of your success», said his father «but do not forget that life contains more than what is contained in books».

24. «What does this mean?» she cried. «Have you brought me bad news?». He replied, «I left our army advancing against the enemy last night. Your army is now winning the battle».

25. «Have you got them?» said the officer. « They are in the cellar under my shop». Tai Sang replied.

26. The speaker said: «Are we to believe his words ? He has often told us lies. Let him prove his statements».

27. «Do you know that it is nearly nine o'clock?» the mother said to the child. «It is time you were in bed».

28. Nemo said to Ali, «Are you interested in machinery?» «**Yes**», said Ali. «I am being trained in the motor-car works». Nemo said, «Come and see, my motor-car».

Exercise 44. Change the following into Indirect Speech

1. «You have my consent», said Orlando. «You can have your wedding to-morrow, Oliver, and I shall invite the duke as well as your friends. Go and persuade your lady to agree to this. She is now alone».

2. What are you doing here?» asked the police man. «That is not your business», replied the stranger. «It will soon be my business», said the policeman «If you loiter much longer outside this jeweller's shop after it is closed. You had better move on».

3. Sir Henry smiled as he said, «The hour is late for a philosophical discussion **lad. I** have letters to write It is a fine night now; leave me alone for a while. Why will you not go for a short walk?».

4. She said to me: «Would you rather ride your own bicycle or borrow mine?».
   I replied, «If you don't mind, I'd rather ride my own».

5. «What do you want?», said Mr. Justice Pantin.
   «I want to talk to you», replied the stranger.
   «I don't think I know you», said the Judge. «Who are you?».
   «I doubt whether my name would mean anything to you», said the man, «because at the moment it is Smith».

Exercise 45. Change into direct speech:

1. The boys shouted with joy that they had won the game.
2. My brother said with sorrow that it was a long time since I had seen him.
3. The engineer asked the workman what he was doing. The latter answered that he had nothing to do for three hours. Then the engineer told him to follow what he himself was busy repairing.
4. The judge asked him by whom he had been robbed and how much he had lost.
5. I asked him who had helped him and when he had arrived and where he was going the next day.
6. I ordered him to do his duty.
7. We advised him not to walk through the wood that night.
8. The beggar prayed the passer-by to give him a piastre.
9. The teacher ordered the pupil to do his work carefully because he would lose marks for carelessness. The pupil answered that he was ready to do his best.
10. The man ordered his son to go to bed early, because they were going to Cairo the next day.
11. The teacher advised the pupil not to be in a hurry and said that if he did, he would be sorry.
12. Tom told Mary that he had never been to the circus and asked her if she would like to go there with him the next day.

JOINING WORDS الروابط

RELATIVE PRONOUNS الاسماء الموصولة

The relative pronouns are used to join sentences together.

تستعمل الاسماء الموصولة لربط الجمل بعضها ببعض ، ولـربط الجمل نتبع الخطوات الآتية : ـ

اولا : نبحث عن كلمة متكررة في الجملة الثانية ثم نبحث عــن موقعها فاذا كانت فاعلا عاقلا نستعمل «WHO» واذا كانت مفعولا به عاقلا نعرف ذلك بوجود الكلمة بعد الفعل فنستعمل «WHOM» واذا كانت غير عاقل نستعمل«WHICH» واذا كانت للملكية نستعمل «WHOSE» واذا احترنا نستعمل كلمة «THAT» ولكننا لا نفضل استعمالها في جميع الاحوال كما يجب ان تلاحظ انها لا تستعمل في الملكية اي بدل «WHOSE»

ثانيا: احذف الكلمة المتكررة من الجملة الثانية وضع الاســـم الموصول والجملة الثانية مباشرة في الجملة الاولى بعد الاســـم الذي حذفت مثله ٠

---

1. «WHO»

تستعمل Who للحلول محل الفاعل العاقل وطبعا يعرف الفاعل بوجوده في اول الجملة ٠٠٠ مثال

1. Here is **the man**. **The man** is a musician.

نحذف كلمة The man من الجملة الثانية ونضع بدلا منها Who ونضع الاسم الموصول والجملة الثانية بعد الكلمة التـي حذفنا مثلها ٠

1. Here is **the man who** is a musician.
2. **The man** came here. **The man** was a musician.
   The man **who was a musician** came here.
3. **My friend** swims well. **He** lives here.
   My friend **who lives** here swims well.

Exercise 46. Join each pair of sentences by means of the relative pronoun «Who»

اربط كل جملتين بواسطة الاسم الموصول

1. I saw a boy. He was sitting on the chair.
2. There are hunters in this town. They live near the forest.
3. The servants were afraid. They thought that there was a ghost in the house.
4. This is the fisherman. He catches fish from the river.
5. The boy went to the doctor. He was ill.
6. Merchants went from town to town. They sold goods.
8. Here is Mary. She cooks well.
9. Every boy has a chance of success. He learns his lessons.
10. The man cut down the tree. He had an axe.
11. Three men were travelling together. They found a purse.
12. The doctor came to see the man. The man was ill
13. The policeman arrested the thief. The thief was leaving the shop.
14. Where is Mary? She is playing tennis.
15. I met the man. He is your brother.
16. You met Zaki. He was crossing the street.
17. This is the boy. He stole my watch.
18. The man is teaching us English. He is an Egyptian.
19. Do you know the teacher? He wrote this book.
20. My sister is reading a book. She is interested in reading.

2. «WHOM»

تستعمل Whom بدلا من المفعول به الذي يعـرف بوجوده
بعد الفعل مثال :

1. **The man** came here. I visited **him.**

نحذف كلمة nim من الجملة الثانية ونضع بدلا منها Whom
في اول الجملة ثم نضع الاسـم الموصول والجمـــــلة الثانية بعد
الكلمة التي حذفنا مثلها ·

   The man whom I visited came here.

2. **The man** was working with me. I paid him.
   The man **whom I paid** was working with me.

ملحوظة اذا اتى قبل المفعول به حرف جر نضع حرف الجر قبل
الاسم الموصول ··· مثل : ــ

3. I have two children.   I am fond of them.
   I have two children **of whom** I am fond.

4. **Ali** came here. I was waiting **for him.**
   Ali **for whom I was waiting** came here.

Exercise 47: Join the following sentences by using «WHOM».

1. The boy is my brother. You saw him.
2. I saw the man. We were waiting for him.
3. The boy had a nice dog. We met him in the garden.
4. Did you see the man? I had spoken to you about him.
5. There are many pupils in the school. We know them.
6. Did you meet the merchant? You bought a motorcar from him.
7. My brother is not in the house. His friend is waiting for him.
8. Amin is my uncle. You know him.
9. Here is the pupil. The teacher is angry from him.
10. I respect the honest man. You work with him.

11. A child was lost in the city. We found him.
12. The boy was ill. The doctor ordered him to stay in bed.
13. Ali was riding a donkey. I met him in the Barrage.
14. He is the leader. We can depend on him.
15. A beggar came to her door. She was kind to him.

3. «WHICH»

تستعمل Which لتحل محل الفاعل او المفعول غير العاقـــل
مثال :

1. He found his book. He lost it yesterday.

نرى ان كلمة it تعود على كلمة his book فنحذفها ونضع بدلا
منها which في اول الجملـة الثانيـة ثـم نضـع الاسـم الموصول
والجملة الثانية بعد الكلمة التي حذف مثلها : ـ

1. He found his book which he lost yesterday.
2. This is the house. I live in it.
   This is the house in which I live.
3. This book is cheap. It is very useful.
   This book which is very useful is cheap.

Exercise 48: Combine each pair of sentences by means of the relative pronoun «WHICH»:

اربط كل جملتين بواسطة الاسم الموصول : ـ

1. The ox was very fat. The butcher killed the ox.
2. You must not eat the fruit. The fruit is unripe.
3. Mary ate the cake. You gave her the cake.
4. He told us a story. It was funny.
5. Our kitchen is clean. We prepare the food in the kitchen.
6. They are in the sitting-room. There are beautiful pictures in it.
7. He gave me a watch. I thanked him for it.
8. The exercise is easy. You asked me to do it.

9. The fountain pen is good. I am writing with it.
10. This is the book. You told me about it.
11. This is the window. He broke it.
12. Did you send the letter? I told you to write it.
13. This is a very difficult exercise. No one can answer it.
14. Tell me your address. It is new.
15. The broken sword does not melt. We shall throw it.

4. THAT

تستعمل that بدلا من الاسماء الموصولة

who - whom - which

اي انها تستعمل بدلا من العاقل وغيـر العاقل فاعلا ومفعولا بــه ٠
ولا تستعمل that مطلقا بدلا من whose

1. The teacher likes **the pupils. They** work hard.
   The teacher likes the pupils **that (who)** work hard.
2. This is **the girl.** You meet **her.**
   This is the girl **that (whom)** you meet.
3. I have **a bird. It** sings.
   I have a bird **that (which)** sings.

ملحوظة : لا تحاول استعمال **THAT** في حل جمل الامتحان بل ابحث عن اسم موصول مناسب ٠ اذ ان المُتحن لا يعتبر **that** اجابة صحيحة تماما ٠

ولذلك فلن نعطيك هنا تمرينات على استعمال **THAT** واتقــــن الاسماء الموصولة الاخرى ٠

5. WHOSE

يستعمل الاسم الموصول WHOSE للاشخاص في حالة الاضافة او حالة الملكية مثل : ـ

1. This is **the man.** I bought **his motor-car.**

هنا نجد كلمة motor-car مملوكة لكلمة the man فنحذف
ضمير الملكية his ونضع بدلا منه الاسم الموصول Whose ولا
تنس ان تضـع بعده كلمة الملكية motor-car ثم ضع الاسم
الموصول وبعده كلمة الملكية وبعدها باقي الجملة الثانية وراء الكلمة
التي حذفنا مثلها : ـ

1. This is the man **whose motor-car I** bought.
2. **The pupil** can not write. **I** have **the pupil's pencil.**
   The pupil **whose pencil I have** can not write.
3. I met **Ali. The watch of Ali** was lost.
   I met Ali whose watch was lost.

Exercise 49: Join by using whose:

1. I met Ali. His bag was lost.
2. I know the man. His brother is an officer.
3. Here is the boy. The boy's father is my friend.
4. The farmer was sad. His dog died.
5. My teacher is good. I succeed with his help.
6. The jeweller became poor. The thieves stole jewels
   from his shop.
7. This is the boy. I borrowed his pen.
8. The men feel warm. Their clothes are made of
   wool.
9. The policeman caught the thief. The thief's leg
   was broken.
10. We comforted the boy. The boy's brother died.
11. I saw a soldier. The arm of the soldier was cut off.
12. Ali felt pain. His finger was cut with a knife.
13. The lady is very kind. Mary lives in her house.
14. Yesterday I visited Maged. His brother came from
    Alex.
15. The boy is very annoyed. A book has been stolen
    from his desk.

GENERAL EXERCISES

Ex. 50: Join the following sentences without using and or but:

1. The tree was cut down. It stood in the middle of the street.
2. The boy broke his arm. The boy jumped out of the window.
3. The man is my uncle. We stayed at the man's house.
4. My father has bought a motor-car. He has paid £500 for it.
5. I saw a dog. The dog was carrying a bone.
6. I met a beautiful girl. The girl had golden hair.
7. I know the man. His son is a doctor.
8. Did you see the girl? I had spoken to you about her.
9. The marks showed the hours. Marks were put on the candles.
10. Many of the men were able to find food. Many of the men came to the Nile Valley.
11. Every year there was a great flood. This flood brought life to all plants.
12. The sheep is living quite happily in some distant country. From its back wool came.
13. The farmer is in the field. We have hired his donkey.
14. Have you met the man? You teach his son.
15. Here are the books. You are looking for them.
16. He has an overcoat. It protects him from cold.
17. Rustum built a splendid palace. He retired to it to spend the rest of his life.
18. She sent a present to her daughter. She loved her dearly.
19. We tried to comfort the woman. The woman's eyes

were full of tears.

B. CONJUNCTIONS   حروف العطف

وحــروف العطــف هــذه كثيــرة سنتوسع في شرحهــا في باب
الـ   Phrase والـ   Clause
ولكن نتعرض في هذا الباب الــى اكثرها استعمالا واهمية في
وصل الجمل بعضها ببعض ٠ وهي :

1. ALTHOUGH   ولو ان

وتستعمل للتناقض أي عندما تكون الجملة الثانية نتيجة غيــر
متوقعة للجملة الاولى ولذلك يوضع حرف العطف هذا امام الجملة
الاولى ٠٠٠ مثال :

He is **poor**. He is **happy**.
Although he is poor, he is **happy**.
He played. He **succeeded**.
Although he played, he succeeded.

Exercise 51 :   - Join these sentences by using « Although » :

1. He is rich. He is unhappy.
2. Mary works hard. She fails.
3. The river is wide. I can cross it.
4. He was given a prize. He did not win the match.
5. There was a war. The Egyptians were not frightened.
6. It was raining. He went out.
7. A metal shines. It is not real gold.
8. He was very hungry. He ate a good meal.
9. Karam learnt his lesson. He did not remember it.
10. The rich man has a motor-car. He never rides it.

2. BECAUSE   بسبب

وتستعمل لبيان السبب من الحدث الاول ولذا فهي توضع قبــل
السبب مثال :

We come to school. We want to learn.
We come to school **because** we want to learn.

Exercise 52. Join these sentences by using«because» :-

1. The child wept. His mother beat him.

2. Mary bought a piece of cloth. She wanted to make a new dress.

3. Karam caught the train. He came early.

4. The pupil made a noise. The teacher punished the pupil.

5. I found no one. They all had gone on a visit.

6. Sami was ill. He stayed at home.

7. I thanked the teacher. He gave me a reward.

8. Amin complained of Nagi. He hit him with a stick.

9. We drink. We are thirsty.

10. You can go now. Your teacher has given you permission.

3. AS SOON AS مجرد	4. WHEN عندما

ويستعمل هذان الحرفان للدلالة علــــى حدوث فعل بمجرد حدوث
فعل آخر ٠٠٠ مثال :

We came. We finished our work.

We came **when** we finished our work.

or: **As soon as** we finished our work we came.

5. WHILE بينما

ويستعمل هذان الحرفان للدلالة عــلى حدوث فعــل بمجرد حدوث
حدث آخر ولا بد من استعمال هذا الحرف اذا كان فعل احـــــــد
انجملتين في الماضي المستمر **Past Continuous**
اذ انت تعلم انه يستعمل بعد while الزمن الماضـي المستمر

Ex: I was walking. I met my friend. **While I was walking I met my friend.**

6.   AFTER بعد

وتستعمل لبيان حدوث فعل بعد فعل آخر وتستعمل After عادة
اذا كان هناك ماضي تام Past Perfect وتوضع في اول جملته .

I had finished my work. I went home.
After I had finished my work, I went home.

Exercise 53 : -
Join by using : «as soon as, when, while, after» : -

1.   The boy was running. He fell down.

2.   The boy went to bed. He had reached home.

3.   It rained. I was returning home.

4.   The mother reached home. Her children ran to meet her.

5.   The man arrived. His friend welcomed him.

6.   Nobody knows the time. The train will arrive at this time.

7.   He had come to school. He entered the class.

8.   Zaki was driving his car. He ran over a child.

9.   I know the time. My friend will come at this time.

10. Nagi ate the cake. He had bought it.

7.   IF   اذا

تستعمل اذا كان هناك سؤال شرط وجواب شرط وتوضع قبل
سؤال الشرط ٠٠٠ مثل : ـ

He works hard. He will succeed.
If he works hard, he will succeed.

Exercise 54 : - Join these sentences by using «If» : -
1.   You will be rich. You work hard.

2. I visit him. He will be pleased.

3. They would win the match. They played well.

4. Kamel eats much. He will be fat.

5. We shall not play football. It rains.

Exercise 55 : -

Join the following sentences without using and or but : -

1. I don't like Fred. He is dishonest.

2. He has never been to college. He is very clever.

3. He works hard. He likes to succeed.

4. He found his watch. He lost it again.

5. He jumped into the river. He wanted to swim to the other bank.

6 We heard the bell. We entered the classroom.

7. He put on a heavy coat. It was very cold.

8. He went to Cairo. He visited his friend. He has not seen him for two years.

9. He was hurt. He fell off his horse.

10. He buys many books. He wants to learn.

11. The roots are crushed. We want to make medicines.

12. Her generosity was very great. She helped everybody who asked for help.

13. The blow was very strong. The knight sank to the ground.

14. The man committed the robbery. He pretended that he had not.

15. The man pretended to be blind. He wished to get money easily.

16. I heard a loud noise. I was studying my lesson.
17. Fatma was careless. She succeeded. She was lucky.
18. He shouted many times. No one heard him.
19. I feel tired. I have worked hard.
20. He ran very fast. He caught the train.
21. He ran very fast. He missed the train.
22. I feel tired. I have not worked hard.
23. He fought bravely. He was defeated.
24. The bell rang. We had gone to our class-rooms.
25. She answered my question. The question was very difficult.

Exercise 56 : - Join each of the following groups of sentences to form one sentence: Do not use «and or but » .

1. Ahmed went home. He had finished his work. It was difficult.
2. The train arrived at the station. I met my friend. I have not seem him for two weeks.
3. The lady was shouting. The thief ran away. He had stolen her bag.
4. The doctor examined him. He ordered him to stay in bed.
5. He was forced to stay in the house. It was raining heavily.
6. Aly's father gave him three pounds every month. He was very wasteful with his money. He was always in debt.
7. Their motor-car broke down ten miles from the

nearest village. The passengers continued on foot. They arrived there at sunset.

8. Aly tried to sell his motor-car to Mohamed . Mohamed refused to buy it. He said that it was too expensive.

9. Watches are the best in the world. They are made in Switzerland. They keep perfect time.

10. Mohamed finished his breakfast quickly. He hurried to the station. He wanted to catch the twelve o'clock train.

11. The workman was repairing the telegraph wire. It was broken. The wind blew very severly the day before yesterday.

12. It rained very hard yesterday. The roads were very muddy. I could not come and see you.

13. I expect to go to England. I succeed in the examination. It will be held next year.

14. Napoleon was a great general. He was conquered in the end. He was fighting against the rest of Europe.

15. The man was hurt in a street accident. He was sent to hospital. He recovered from his hurts in it.

PHRASE AND CLAUSE

KINDS OF SENTENCES   انواع الجمل

الجمل ثلاث انواع

1. Simple   بسيطة
2. Compound   مركبة
3. Complex   معقدة

1. I saw a boy. He was riding a bicycle.

هذه جمل بسيطة Simple لانها تحتوي على فعل واحد

2. I saw a boy and he was riding a bicycle.

هذه جملة مركبة Compound لانها مركبة من جملتين احداهما
بسيطة يمكن الفصل بينهما وتدل كل منهما على معنى مستقل ·

3. I saw a boy who was riding a bicycle.

جملة معقدة Complex لانها تحتوي على اكثر من فعل وهي مركبة
من جملة اساسية Principal clause (I saw a boy)
وجملة متعلقة بها subordinate clause وهي التي تبدأ من حرف
الوصل (who was riding a bicycle)

HOW TO JOIN SIMPLE SENTENCES
INTO ONE SIMPLE SENTENCE

كيفية وصل الجمل البسيطة الى جملة واحدة بسيطة · اي تحتوي
على فعل واحد   A simple sentence has one verb only.
There are four ways to join sentences into one simple
sentence.

هناك اربع طرق لوصل الجمل الى جملة واحدة بسيطة وهي :ـ

1. By using an adjective   ١ ـ باستعمال صفة
2. By using a participle.   ٢ ـ باستعمال اسم المفعول

٣ ـ باستعمال حرف جر مع الاسم او مع اسم المفعول

3. **By using a preposition with a noun or participle.**

4. **By using the infinitive.**   ٤ ـ باستعمال المصدر

---

1. **By using adjectives.**
   The boy was young. He lost his book. It was **new.**
   He lost it **yesterday.**
   The **young** boy lost his **new** book **yesterday.**

2. **By using present participe   (ing + الفعل)**
   I sat at the window. I saw Aly. He was crossing the street.
   Sitting at the window, I saw Aly **crossing** the street.

3. **By using a preposition with present participle or noun.**
   He succeeds. He works hard.
   He succeeds by **working** hard.
   He succeeds with **hard work.**

4. **By using infinitive.**   باستعمال المصدر
   He went to Alex. He visited his uncle.
   He went to Alex to visit his uncle.

Exercise 57 : - Join these sentences to make one sentence in each case, having only one verb : -

1. The cup was broken beyond repair. It lay in shining pieces on the floor.

2. He took his spoon. He began to eat.

3. Join these sentences. Do not use and or but.

4. You have been disobedient. You cannot come with us to the barrage.

5. Sadly I read the report. He had been killed in a railway accident.

6. The insects were very numerous. They covered the field with their bodies.
7. Mary finished her breakfast. She hurried to the station. She wanted to catch the train.
8. Aly got up early. He **came** to school. He walked slowly.
9. Karam **went** home. Karam finished his work. It was difficult.
10. I saw Sami. He was coming to school. It was a rainy day.

THE COMPOUND SENTENCE

A compound sentence consists of two or more complete statements, all of equal importance:

تتركب الجملة المركبة من جملتين تامتين او اكثر كلها ذات اهمية متساوية .

1. The conjunctions used are: And (و) (لكي) but

تستعمل «and» لربط جملتيـن بينهما صلة في المعنى ولكل منهما علاقة ورابطة بالاخرى .

She was thirsty and drank some water.

تستعمل «but» لربط جملتين بينهما تناقض واختلاف في المعنى اي ان تكون الجملة الثانية خلاف ما يتوقعه الانسان من الجمـلـة الاولى .

He is polite but his brother is rude.

2. «Not only......but also» joins two statements and emphasizes the second.

تربط جملتين اخباريتين وتؤكـد الجملة الثانية

He works hard. He finds time to play.
Not only does he work hard but he **also** finds time to play.

من هذه الجملة الثانية نرى انه اذا اتت ... Not only في اول
الجملة فعاملها كما لو كانت استفهام اي ضع الفعل قبل الفاعل

He is rich. He is happy.

Not only is he rich but also he is happy.

He is not only rich but also he is happy.

3. «Either .... or» تستعمل للتعبير عن التفضيل بين شيئين

Either you must work harder or you will fail.

4. «Neither...... nor» (joins two negative statements).

تستعمل لربط جملتين منفيتين

She is not beautiful. She is not rich.

She is neither beautiful nor she is rich.

اذا اتت Neither في اول الجملةفعاملها كما لو كانت استفهام اي
ضع الفعل قبل الفاعل

Neither is she beautiful nor she is rich.

Exercise 58. Combine the following sentences in order to make one compound sentence :

1. He spoke clearly. He told the truth.
2. Some people cannot read. They cannot write.
3. The man was a thief. He was innocent.
4. He broke his promise. He told a lie.
5. He can drive a motor-car. He can ride a horse well.
6. There is not ink. There is not chalk in the classroom.
7. The door was left open. It was opened from outside.
8. Mary is clever. She is a hard worker.
9. Cotton clothes are pretty. They are cheap.
10. There was a strom. The ship was saved.
11. He likes apples. He is fond of oranges.
12. He pays the debt. He will be put in prison.
13. Those boys are not clever. They are not careful.

14. Your friend is a doctor. He is a teacher.
15. Ali went home. He lay in bed.
16. The thief was caught. He was put in prison.
17. You must work hard. Your father will be angry with you.
18. Our army was small. He conquered the English army.
19. She cannot cook. She cannot wash.
20. Mary was kind to the beggar. She gave him clothes.

THE COMPLEX SENTENCE
الجملة المعقدة

A complex sentence consists of one principal statement and one or more subordinate clauses.

تتكون الجملة المعقدة من جزء اساسي وجزء متعلق

(Principal Clause) I read several books/while I was ill (subordinate clause).

Subordinate clauses are of three kinds:

والجزء المتعلق قد يكون احد انواع ثلاثة

1. Noun clause.   2. Adjectival clause.   3. Adverbial clause.

Phrases and clauses:

A phrase : is a combination of words, forming part of the sentence but **without a verb.**

مجموعة كلمات تكوّن جزءا مـــن الجملة بدون فعل ٠٠٠ مثــل : ـ

1. I saw a man **carrying a stick.**
2. **The book on the table** is mine.

A clause : is a combination of words **containing a verb.**

مجموعة كلمات تحوي فعلا ٠٠٠ مثل : ـ

1. I saw a man **who was carrying a stick.**
2. The book **which is on the table** is mine.

---

1. NOUN CLAUSE

The noun clause does the work of a noun.

جملة فيها فعل حلت محل اسم

للتغيير من phrase الى clause اتبع الخطوات الآتية :

١ ـ حرف وصل مناسب   ٢ ـ فعل وفاعل

حروف الوصل هي : ـ   Who, whose, whom, which, what, when, where, how, why, or that

1. **His return** is certain. **(Phrase)**
   That he returns is certain. **(N. Clause)**

2. Express **your thoughts** clearly. **(Phrase)**
   Express **what you think** clearly. **(N. Clause)**

ملحوظة : ـ يجب ان تراعي تتابع الازمنة بمعنى اذا كان الفعل الاساسي ماضيا فالفعل الجديد يكون ماضيا ٠

Exercise 59 : Expand the following sentences by changing the black typed words into Noun Clauses :

1. Tell me **your address.**
2. He refused to carry out **my command.**
3. We must hope **for your success.**
4. We know **the maker of the chair.**
5. He did not hear **of the death of his father.**
6. He died **at the age of sixty.**
7. He was afraid **of failure.**
8. I met **the builder of the house.**
9. Write down **your age.**
10. None knew **her weight.**
11. Mary told me **about her marriage.**
12. I congratulated him **on his speech.**

13. Can you tell me **the height of the Pyramid?**
14. She knows **the way to make sweets.**
15. Do you know **the price of this shoe?**
16. Karam forgot **his birth place.**
17. None knows **the reason for his absence.**
18. A father buys **the wants of his son.**
19. No one knows **the depth of the sea.**
20. I heard **of his arrival** to Cairo.

للتغيير من Noun Clause الى Phrase اتبع الخطوات
الآتية : ـ
١ ـ احذف اداة الربط (حرف الاستفهام او كلمة that)
٢ ـ احذف الفاعل
٣ ـ هات اسما

Exercise 60 : Rewrite these sentences using nouns or phrases instead of the noun clause in black type:

1. Bring **what is necessary** with you.
2. Do not forget **where your examination will be.**
3. My father knows **how wide this room is.**
4. He did not tell me **why he came.**
5. Mary knows **what the meaning of this word is.**
6. I was glad to hear **that he succeeded.**
7. Do you know **how far it is between the earth and the moon?**
8. We agreed **to what he said.**
9. Ali told me **how much his book costs.**
10. Tell the teacher **how many boys there are in the class.**
11. The mother knows **why her child is weeping.**
12. The applicant wrote down **where he lived.**
13. Huda knows **how she can make cakes.**
14. Every woman lies about **how old she is.**
15. **What he described of the battle** was right.

2. ADJECTIVAL CLAUSE

جملة فيها فعل حلت محل صفة

An adjectival clause **describes** a noun

للتغيير من Pnrase الى Clause اتبع نفس الخطوات
السابق اتباعها في Noun clause وهي : ـ

١ ـ هات حرف وصل مناسبا وحروف الوصل هي : ـ

The conjunctions are :

Who, whom, whose, which, that.

**« That » can be used instead of (who, whom,
which) but it cannot be used instead of «whose».**

تستعمل كلمة that بدلا من اي حرف وصل ولكنها لا تستعمـــل
بدلا من whose

٢ ـ هات فعلا وعادة هو احد اجزاء «Verb to be» اي
am, is, are, was, were

ولا تنس تتــابع الازمنة أي أن يطـــابق الفعل الثــاني الفعل الاصلي
سواء اكان مضارعا او ماضيا .

٣ ـ ثم ضع الصفة مثل : ـ

The **rich** man spends his money foolishly. (Adjective)
The man **who is rich** spends his money foolishly. (Adjectival clause)
I like **well-cooked** food. (Adjective)
I like food **which is well-cooked**. (Adjectival clause)

Exercise 61 : Expand the following from simple sentences into complete sentences containing adjectival clauses :

1. The boat **on the river** has no sail.
2. Stones, **lying on the road**, are dangerous.
3. Every boy **in this class** must work hard.
4. The **Alexandria** train will leave at four o'clock.

5. The goods **in the shop window** were damaged by fire.

6. The petrol **found in Egypt** is large in quantity.

7. I like to have a house **surrounded with a garden**.

8. The woman **carrying a basket** sells oranges.

9. The **clever** girl succeeds every year.

10. A **mad** dog bit my **little** brother.

11. In winter we put on **woollen** clothes.

12. The soldier **with one arm** cannot fight well.

13. Mary has a garden full of **beautiful** flowers.

14. I admire **the writer of this book**.

15. We believe the **honest** man.

16. The **dead** man was buried in grave.

17. The **brave** men defended Egypt.

18. Sami wrote **an interesting** story.

19. The passengers **in the train** were injured in the accident.

20. A **clever** boy must depend on himself in answering a difficult question.

لتغير الـ Adjectival Clause الى Phrase اتبع الخطوات الآتية :

١ ـ احذف حرف الوصل   ٢ ـ احذف الفعل

٣ ـ ضع الصفة قبل الموصوف   مثل : ـ

The man **who is rich** is happy.

The **rich** man is happy.

Exercise 62 : Rewrite these sentences using adjectives or phrases instead of the adjectival clauses in black type :

1. The man **who is poor** has no food.

2. The boy **who is clever** answers the exercise which is **difficult**.

3. Brids **which are beautiful** build nests of straw.

4. The girl **who was careless** did not write the exercise.
5. I have a servant **who is honest.**
6. Karam bought a book **which had a red cover.**
7. Mary puts on clothes **which are made of silk.**
8. The boy **who is little cannot join the army.**
9. The soldier **who was brave** shot the aeroplane.
10. Fatma cooks food **which is sweet.**

---

3. THE ADVERBIAL CLAUSE

The adverbial clause does the work of an adverb.
An adverbial clause may be a clause of :

1. **Purpose** غرض
2. **Consequence or Result** نتيجة
3. **Cause** سبب
4. **Time** زمن
5. **Comparison** مقارنة
6. **Manner** حال
7. **Concession or contrast** تناقض
8. **Condition** شرط

1. CLAUSE OF PURPOSE الغرض

The conjunctions are: ـ : حروف الوصل هي
a) **That, so that,** لكي **in order that**
يتبعها **may** في المضارع او **might** في الماضي
b) **lest** (in order that not, for fear that) . . . .
should. يتبعهـــا

Example :

1. He **ran** so that he **might** catch the train.
2. He is running so that be **may** catch the train.
3. He **ran** lest he **should** miss the train.

Exercise 63 :   Complete with a clause of purpose :
1. The thief ran away lest ....
2. People buy books so that ....
3. The teacher spoke clearly in order that ....
4. We have come to school so that ....
5. Everyone works hard in order that ....
6. He saved his money so that ....
7. I lent him five pounds lest ....
8. You must calculate very carefully lest ....
9. Mary got up early in order that ....
10. He went home so that ....
11. They have put hats on their heads in order that..
12. Karam told me a funny story so that ....
13. The child's mother was anxious lest ....
14. I invited my friends to my house in order that ...
15. Pupils go to the library in order that ....

──────────────

للتغيير الى Phrase اتبع الخطوات الآتية : ـ

١ ـ احذف حرف وصل الـ Clause وضع حرف وصل الـ Phrase
٢ ـ احذف الفاعل   ٣ ـ حروف وصل الـ Phrase هي
To ·· in order to, so as to, in the hope of +الفعل + ing
with the aim of + الفعل + ing.

٤ ـ حروف وصل الـ phrase بدلا من lest هي : ـ
for fear of + الفعل + ing. او so as not to

1.   He ran **so that he might** catch the train. (Clause)
   He ran **to (in order to, so as to)** catch the train.

2.   He is running **in order that he may catch** the train.
   He is running **with the aim of catching** the train.

3.   He ran **lest he should** miss the train.
   He ran **so as not to miss** the train. Or : He ran **for**

fear of missing the train.

Exercise 64 : Change this into phrase, and Vice Versa:

1. We went to Alexandria in order that we might enjoy fresh air.
2. He works hard so that he may succeed.
3. He took his spoon to eat.
4. We went to the garden in order to breathe fresh air.
5. They worked hard for fear of failing.
6. Karam went to the cinema to see the film.
7. We go to school with the aim of learning.
8. He bought a fountain pen to write with.
9. Certain drugs are used in order to kill the cotton worm.
10. He went to his house so that he might meet us.
11. She sleeps early lest she should be late.
12. We all work in order that we may eat.
13. The teacher watched the pupils very carefully lest someone should cheat.
14. Do your duty lest you should be punished.
15. Boys play football to be strong.

2. CLAUSE OF RESULT النتيجة

حروف الوصل that اسم موصوف Such , that صفة So

اي نضع بعد so اسما ، وبعد such اسما موصوفا

٢ _ اذا اتت so او such في اول الجملة ضع الفعل قبل الفاعل

1. **He is so clever that** he can answer any question.
2. **He is such a clever boy that** he can answer any question.
3. **So clever is he that** he can answer any question.
4. **Such a clever boy is he that** he can answer any question.

Exercise 65.   Complete with Clause of Result: -

1. It was so dark that ....
2. The load is so heavy that ....
3. Such a lazy boy ....
4. He is such a good player ....
5. So afraid was he that ....
6. So clearly did he speak that ....
7. Such a noise did he make that ....
8. Such a polite boy was he that ....
9. Karam was so tired ....
10. Mary wrote such answers ....
11. He is so ill that ....
12. So many mistakes did he make ....
13. I was so relieved to hear ....
14. There was such a shower of rain that ....
15. The policeman struck the thief so hard ....

للتغيير من Clause of result الى Phrase اتبع الخطوات الآتية : ـ

١ ـ احذف اداة ربط الـ Clause وهات اداة ربط الـ Phrase وهي
...... enough to في حالـة الاثبات to ...... too في حالة النفي

٢ ـ ضع الصفة قبل enough to وبين كلمتين to ...... too
مثال

1. He is **so clever that** he can answer any question:
   He is **clever enough** to answer any question.

2. He is **so lazy that** he cannot answer any question.
   He is **too lazy to** answer any question.

Exercise 66 : -

Change the following into phrase - and vice verse:

1. Tom is too ill to go to school.
2. Mary was too clever to make silly mistakes.
3. The boy was so frightened that he could not move.
4. She is such a good girl that everyone praised her.
5. He was too weak to swim any more.
6. I was too tired to go with him.
7. The baby is too young to walk.
8. The time was so short that we could not answer the exercise.
9. Ali is such a poor man that he cannot buy food.
10. The bag was so heavy that the porter could not carry it.

3. CLAUSE OF CONCESSION OR CONTRAST التناقض

وفيها الحدث الثاني نتيجة عكسية وتناقض للحدث الاول
The conjunctions are :   حروف الوصل هي :

1. **Although, though**   = ولو
2. **However**   مهما + صفة   **adjective or adverb.**
3. **Whatever**   مهما + **Noun** اسم

1. Although he is poor, he is happy.
2. However wide the river is, he can cross it.
3. Whatever help you give him, he will not thank you.

Phrase حروف وصل ال
In spite of, For all, Notwithstanding, despite.

1. **In spite of**   الاسم +
2. **In spite of**   + الفعل +   **ing.**

1. Notwithstanding his poverty, he is happy.
   In spite of being poor, he is happy.
2. In spite of the width of the river, he can cross it.
   In spite of being wide, he can cross the river.
3. For all your help to him, he will not thank you.
   In spite of giving him help, he will not thank you.

Exercise 67 : - Complete with a Clause of Contrast.

1. He did not answer the questions although ....
2. Though he was ill ....
3. Whatever mistake you make ....
4. However careful you may be ....
5. Although I warned him many times ....

6. However rich ....

7. Whatever you do ....

8. Though the policeman hurried ....

9. ...... though he was very skilful.

10. However hard the enemy resists ....

11. Although shoes are polished often ....

12. He would not come whatever ....

13. Although the boy is young ....

14. In spite of his bravery ....

15. Although he was very well educated ....

Exercise 68: - Change into phrase and vice versa : -

1. In spite of all her talk, she has done nothing.

2. I believe you whatever lies you tell.

3. He will always be miserable whatever money he earns.

4. In spite of running quickly, he could not catch the thief.

5. In spite of coming by taxi, we came late.

6. **In spite of his laziness** he passed the examination.

7. **Despite his poverty** he was happy.

8 **Notwithstanding his hard work** he failed.

9. **However loud his voice was** I heard nothing.

10. **Whatever books he reads** he understands nothing.

11. In spite of being cold, I feel quite warm.

12. He defeated the champion in spite of his small size .

13. The prisoner escaped notwithstanding the precautions of the police.

14. He has little to show for all his hard work.

15. In spite of my advice, he continued to make mistakes.

4. CLAUSE OF CAUSE السبب

because, since, as, for. : حروف الوصل
He ate **because** he was hungry.
He drank **since** he was thirsty.

ملحوظة : نفرق في هذا النوع بعدم وجود مضـــــارع since :
قبلها مثلما هو في Clause of time اذ نلاحظ دائما تتابع ازمنة

Phrase حروف الـ

1. Due to   2. Owing to
3. On account of   4. Through

ing + الفعل + **because of** او الاسم + **because of** – ٥
في اول الجملة ing + الفعل – ٦

1. He ate **because of** his hunger.
    He ate **because of** being hungry.
    Being hungry, he ate.

2. He drank **owing to** his thirst.
    He drank **on account** of being thirsty.
    Being thirsty, he drank.

Exercise 69 : - Complete with a clause of cause : -

1. He was barefoot because ....
2. The motor-car stopped because ....
3. He was unfortunate as ....
4. We kill the flies because ....

5. He was puzzled as ....

Exercise 70 : - Change into phrase and vice versa : -

1. Because he was young, he did not join the army.
2. He stayed at home as he was ill.
3. Mary studies her lessons easily since she is clever.
4. He was able to buy a motor-car as he was rich.
5. I admire this king **because he treats his subjects kindly.**
6. I like this boy **on account of his respectfulness of his parents.**
7. I dislike this man **because of his ill humour.**
8. This boy failed in the exmination **due to his carelessness.**
9. This boy succeded **through his cleverness.**
10. I am safe **because you help me.**
11. On account of the teacher's severity, the class sat silent.
12. Due to his foolishness, many people were injured.
13. Owing to the doctor's skill, the man's life was saved.
14. The boats could not cross the river because the flood was fearful.
15. The swiminer could not cross the river because the current was rapid.

5. CLAUSE OF TIME الزمن

The conjunctions are : - حروف الوصل هي :

1. When عندما until حتى till حتى as soon as مجرد
2. While + was او were + الفعل + ing
3. Since + ماضي بسيط ⇐ مضارع تام
4. No sooner had .... than. (ما كاد ٠٠ حتى)
5. Hardly had .... than.
6. Before (before) نضع الفعل الذي قبل كلمة في الماضي التام
7. After ....

نضع الفعل بعد كلمة (after) في الماضي التام ونضع الفعــل الآخر في الماضي البسيط

٨ ـ للتغيير الى phrase استعمل

ing + حرف الوصل, till, until, after, before+ الاسم او الفعل,
او On + الاسم او الفعل + ing (وخاصة مع
no sooner had since, as soon)

او In, during + الفعل + ing في اول الجملة ٠

Examples of Clauses and Phrases of Time :

1. **When he entered** the room he sat down.
   Entering the room he sat down.

2. **After I had put my books** in the desk, **I went out** .

   Having put my books in the desk, **I went out.**

3. I refused to speak **when he was present.**
   I refused to speak **in his presence.**

4. **As soon as the thief saw the policeman,** he took to his heels.

   (On) seeing the policeman , the thief took to his heels.

5. **While I was walking** in the street, I met Fuad.

While (on) walking in the street, I met Fuad.

6. **While the teacher was absent,** we did not have a lesson.
During the teacher's absence, we did not have a lesson.

7. We have not heard of them **since they departed.**
We have not heard of them **since their departure.**

8. I had eaten my breakfast **before I came to school.**
I had eaten my breakfast **before coming to school.**

9. **After he had finihed** his work, he went for a walk.
After finishing his work, he went for a walk.
or **Having finished** his work, he went for a walk.

10. We shall wait **until he arrives.**
We shall wait **until his arrival.**

11. **No sooner had he gone home,** than I came.
On his going home, I came.

Exercise 71 : - Complete with a clause of time: -

1. As soon as ...... the audience applauded.

2. Do not write until ....

3. ...... since he left for Alex.

4. While he was climbing over a fence ....

5. When the train arrived ....

6. The mother sent for the doctor when ....

7. Since cotton was cultivated in Egypt, farmers ....

8. No sooner had the thief seen the policeman ......

9. No sooner had he got better ....

10. The boys ran for shelter as soon as ....

11. Karam has never offered Ali a cigarette since....

12. The man trembled with fear when ....

13. While he was playing ....

14. After he had seen the time table ....

15. No sooner had the fisherman cast his net ....

Exercise 72: - Change into clause and vice versa: -

1. On walking in the street, I met Mary.

2. Before coming to school, I had eaten my breakfast

3. After reaching home, we went to bed.

4. While I was opening the door, I heard a bell ringing.

5. After they had mounted the donkey, they continued their journey.

6. No sooner had he written his exercise than he went home.

7. Karam had gone home before he succeeded.

8. You have much to do before departure.

9. He departed after his succees.

10. On seeing him I ran.

11. **While he was absent** they played.

12. I shall wait **until you return.**

13. I have not seen him **since he returned.**

14. I fell senseless and **when I became conscious again** I was lying in bed.

15. **When the cat is away,** the mice play.

16. **No sooner had they settled in** than the weather

turned nasty.

17. **As soon as he heard the child's moan, he telephon-**ed the doctor to come.

18. **Immediately on the teacher's enterance, the pupi-**ls sat down quietly.

19. He refused to say anything **in her presence.**

20. **On looking out of the window,** I saw Ali coming.

6. CLAUSE OF CONDITION الشرط

If, اذا **unless (if not)** : حروف الوصل
If + present **→** shall, will **+** verb
If **+** past **→** should, would + verb
If + past perfect **→** should have, would have **+**

participle

1. **If he works** hard, he **will** succeed.

2. **If he worked** hard, he would **succeed.**

3. **If he had worked** hard, he **would have succeeded.**

4. **Unless** he had worked hard, he would have **failed.**

للتغيير الى phrase استعمل بدلا من if
with + او الاسم **for** + الفعل + **ing**

1. **For working hard** he will succeed.

2. **With his hard work he would** have succeeded.

but for + verb الفعل + ing: unless واستعمل بدلا من
without + Noun أو الاسم
Unless he worked hard, he would fail.
But for working hard, he would fail.
Unless he had worked hard, he would have failed.
Without his hard work, he would have failed.

OMISSION of IF حذف

لتحسين الاسلوب نحذف **If** ونضع بدلا منها في اول الجملة

Had ⟫⟶ should have, would have + past participle

$$\left.\begin{array}{l}\textbf{Should} \\ \textbf{Were}\end{array}\right\} \longleftarrow \textbf{should, would + verb}$$

Had he come, he would have understood.
Should she come, she would understand.
Were I a bird, I should fly all over the world.

Exercise 73 :- Complete :-

1. Had I enough money ......

2. You will succeed but only if ......

3. Unless you go away ......

4. Unless Mary comes early

5. If I had not helped him ......

6. If he was not lazy ......

7. Had he not worked well ......

8. If he runs, he ......

9. If you told us funny stories, we ......

10. If the house had fallen, ...

11. Unless you obey me, you ......

12. If he tells the truth, ...

13. If the servant broke the glass, ...

14. If the man had gone there, he ......

15. If they demand money by force ......

16. The teacher would not excuse the pupil if ......

17. If you make a trip to the oasis ......

18. Had he been rich . . . . . .
19. Unless he was innocent . . . . . .
20. Should snow fall this summer . . . .
21. If he ran fast . . . . . .
22. . . . . . . he would not have been punished.
23. The grocer refused to deliver the goods unless. . . .
24. Should he come now . . . . . .
25. Had I known his address . . . . . .

Exercise 74 : - Change into phrase and vice-versa :-

1. If he had not been lazy, he would have passed easily.
2. If you do not speak, I shall leave the room.
3. Unless he tries harder he will fall.
4. **Without your doing this** you will get into trouble.
5. If it rained, we should stay indoors.
6. **The weather being fine, I** shall go to the match.
7. **Without his freedom** he can tell nothing.
8. **With or without his permission I** should go.
9. **If he fails** his father will punish him.
10. Without your help he would have drowned.
11. Without money, we cannot travel to Europe.
12. We cannot live without food.
13. If we had not helped him, he would have died of hunger.
14. Unless you do this, you will not get a reward.
15. If you are careful, you will avoid many mistakes.
16. **If he gives me permission or not,** I shall leave the room.
17. He would be very thankful, **if he could be helped in all his troubles.**
18. If he confesses, he will be set free.

19. If Mary had written the exercise carefully, she would have taken a good mark.
20. Unless you obey your mother, she will become angry with you.

7. CLAUSE OF MANNER : الحالة او الكيفية

حروف الوصل :

The conjunctions are : — as — as if — as though.
(Notice): The last two conjunctions take «WERE» if the principal verb is **present** and take «HAD BEEN» if the principal verb is **past**).

were **as if, as though** حرفا الوصل نضع مع الفعل
had been اذا كان الفعل الاخر مضارعا ونضع الفعل بعدهما
اذ كان الفعل الاخر ماضيا •

Ex. 1. He **behaves** as if (as though) he **were** a great man.
2. He **behaved** as if (as though) he **had been** a great man.

للتغيير الى Phrase استعمل

Phrase: look like - to be like in ......ing, according to.
He looks like a great man in behaving.
He is like a great man in behaving.

Exercise 75 :- Complete by adding a clause of manner:

1. Do as ......
2. He spoke as if ......
3. The porter pushes the heavy box as if ......
4. He ran away as though ......
5. She was stupid as if ......

Exercise 76 :- Change into phrase and vice-versa :-

1. He held the pen **according to the teacher's** instructions.

2. He entered the hall in a kingly manner.
3. According to the order of the police, you must not leave your car in this place.
4. According to his good luck, he escaped punishment.
5. He was like a leader in walking.
6. Karam looked like a lion in fighting.
7. Everything happened as I hoped.
8. The house was built as he ordered.
9. Mary looks like her mother in cooking.
10. The carpenter worked as if he had been skilful.

GENERAL EXERCISES

Exercise 77 :- Complete :-

1. Although the examination is easy ......
2. He stayed at home till ......
3. I went to Cairo so that ......
4. Had I not wasted my time, ...
5. If you give us something to eat ......
6. He listened eagerly to the teacher so that ......
7. No sooner had he found his watch ......
8. You ought to make haste lest ......
9. The engineer pulled down the old house lest......
10. No sooner had the whistle sounded ......
11. The more the pupil works ......
12. We should welcome tourists to our country so that ......
13. I gave the waiter a tip **after** ......
14. **The more** you eat ......
15. The boy was **so intelligent** ......

16. **No sooner had** the mother covered the baby ......
17. **Although** we heard many stories about Ali ......
18. **The more** money you spend ......
19. **If** he takes the medicine regularly ......
20. **Unless the man is careful about his money** ......
21. **Had** the merchant not been able to borrow ......
22. **If you** do not give him a recommendation ......
23. **Since** he was elected ......
24. This bag is **so heavy** ......
25. **If** she **had obeyed** her mother ......

Exercise 78: Rewrite the following sentences beginning with the words between brackets: make any necessary changes:-

1 He found his watch, but he lost it again. (No sooner).
2. I should have eaten something if I had felt hungry. (Had)
3. Unless he tries harder he will fail. (If)
4. In spite of his illness he came to school (Although)
5. Immediately after our getting into the train, it began to move. (No sooner).
6. In spite of his wealth, he is unhappy. (However).
7. Although he was clean, he caught illness (In spite of).
8. After she had covered him, she heard a knock on the door. (No sooner).
9. She did not finish her work though I helped her. (In spite of).
10. As soon as he entered the room, the lights went out. (No sooner).
11. He was too lazy to work. (So)

12. But for his bravery, he would run away. (Unless).
13. They have become so real to me that I regard them as my personal friends. (So).
14. In spite of his stupidity, he succeeded. (Although)
15. He is so polite that we all like him. (Such).

Exercise 79 : Join to make a complex sentence :-

1. I have not seen him. He came back from Europe.
2. The whole family collected. They wanted to say goodbye to their son.
3. The sportsman took up his gun. The gun was lying in the corner of the hall. He went out after a tiger.
4. Lamp-black is used in paints and boot polishes. It is one of the products obtained from coal.
5. The engineers heightened the dam. They wanted to increase our water-supply. (Purpose)
6. The thief ran very quickly. He escaped from his pursuers. (Result).
7. First the foundations are made. Then the builders begin to erect the walls. (Time).
8. The price of these motor-cars is low. We have not sold many of them. (Concession).

Exercise 80. Change into clause :-

1. The teacher punished **the disobedient pupil.**
2. **Having heard that,** he became very angry.
3. The donkey began to show **its displeasure.**
4. Some little boys marched in front **to clear the way.**
5. They met a traveller **walking along the road.**
6. **In spite of his illness,** he went to work as usual.
7. **Without money,** we cannot buy anything.
8. **On his death,** Saladin took his place.
9. Ali was too ill to move.

10. Everybody liked him because of his gratitude to his parents.

11. In spite of my warning, he carried out the journey.

12. Immediately on his appearance he was shot.

13. On seeing us they refused to come into the room.

14. Ali saw **a flying** ball in the sky.

15. The servant found his **murdered** master in his bed.

16. (Because of his good luck) he escaped punishment.

17. (Hearing the tale), they went to sleep.

18. (In spite of his advice) they went on the journey.

19. (Having no money to buy food), the man slept without supper.

20. I could make out who was there (in spite of the darkness).

Exercise 81 : Change into phrase :-

1. He answered this question **because he was intelligent.**

2. **As I was tired,** I lay down.

3. He stayed at home till I returned.

4. The boys saw no reason why they should wait.

5. Although he was brave, he was easily **beaten.**

6. Nobody respected him because he was an ignorant man.

7. Although he was clever, he was not given any reward.

8. Although she worked hard, she was unfortunate.

9. Although I assisted him, he failed to answer correctly.

10. We all work in order that we may eat.

11. **As I came to the top of the hill** I saw a little **town** below.

12. The coffee was **so hot that I could not drink it.**

ANSWERS

Exercise 1 :
1) a 2) an 3) a 4) an 5) an.

Exercise 2 :
1) am 2) is 3) are 4) are 5) is.

Exercise 3 :
1) has 2) has 3) have 4) have 5) has.

Exercise 4 :
1) shall 2) will 3) shall 4) will 5) will.

Exercise 5 :
1) Do 2) Does 3) Do 4) Does 5) Do.

Exercise 6 :
1) spend 2) does 3) marches,does 4) go
5) are, are 6) pass 7) shines 8) go
9) helps, ask 10) leave 11) rains.

Exercise 7 :
1) made 2) bought 3) sold 4) played
5) succeeded 6) saw, asked, was 7) went, wanted
8) did not visit, was 9) found 10) forgave.

Exercise 8 :
1) will read 2) shall learn 3) shall go
4) shall give 5) shall visit.

Exercise 9 :
1. is she doing, is making.
2. are they doing, are writing.
3. is cooking.
4. are playing.
5. am writing.
6. is sowing.
7. is playing.
8. am answering.
9. is building.
10. is your brother going.

Exercise 10 :

1. was crossing, met.
2. saw, was walking.
3. was moving, jumped.
4. was sleeping, came.
5. were working, knock-
ed.
6. saw, was driving.
7. were working, came.
8. was going, met.
9. was escaping, fell.
10. searched, was wait-
·ing.
11. shouted, was study-
ing.
12. was sleeping, broke.

Exercise 11 :

1. followed, has improv-
ed.
2. have just caught.
3. has already permit-
ted.
4. asked, have done.
5. have been, offered.
6. have been discovered.
7. has lately been ap-
pointed.
8. have not heard, left.
9. has just drawn.
10. has not yet rung.
11. has never left, was.
12. has run.
13. have obeyed, was.
14. have lost.
15. has already left.

Exercise 12 :

1. had left, came.
2. had finished, went.
3. returned, had spent.
4. had written, sent.
5. had stolen, ran.
6. found, had lost.
7. ate, had bought.
8. had left, arrived.
9. told, had seen.
10. had been taken, ar-
rived.
11. beat, had bitten.
12. began, had rung.
13. had died, arrived.
14. had written, started.
15. lived, had bought.

Exercise 13 :

1. shall return.
2. may arise.
3. should miss.
4. should lose.
5. should punish.
6. had made.
7. will not pay.
8. would have not won.
9. might learn.
10. may enjoy.

Exercise 14 :

Tell, told, told. **Lead,** led, led. **Cost,** cost, cost. **Lay,** laid, laid. **Teach,** taught, taught. **Sweep,** swept, swept. **Dream,** dream, dreamt or **dream,** dreamed, dreamed. **Pay,** paid, paid. **Hurt,** hurt, hurt. **Grow,** grew, grown.**Bite,** bit, bitten. **Weave,** wove, woven. **Fight,** fought, fought. **Buy,** bought, bought. **Spread,** spread, spread.

Exercise 15 .

1. awoke, had shone.
2. was playing, fell, broke.
3. has not yet begun.
4. had gone, came, stole.
5. have not seen, left.
6. has just rung.
7. stole, has been frightened.
8. had gone, heard, was expected has studied.
9. was running, fell, hurt, saw lying, had spoilt.
10. have been taught, shall go.

Exercise 16 :

1. lost, forgotten, shall bring.
2. will set the prisoner free.
3. left, had rung.
4. drives.
5. bought.

Exercise 17 :

Tore, happened, was playing, knocked, became, began, was, seized, escape, twisted, fled, leaping, was caught, tore.

Exercise 18 :

1. am, is.
2. went, bought.
3. shall visit, will take.
4. gets, goes.
5. dropped, was working.
6. months, found, had lost.
7. began, has not yet written.
8. had paid, gave.
9. felt, was flying, hight.
10. did you go.
11. have not seen.
12. is playing.
13. caught, was trying.
14. had kissed, went.
15. sees, will run.

Exercise 19 :

1. bought.
2. saw, went.
3. dresses.
4. go.
5. runs.
6. went, took.
7. rises.
8. was running.
9. left, have not received.
10. bought, had sold.
11. answer, will make.
12. were writing, entered.
13. shall go, shall swim.
14. was waving, started.
15. has been.
16. rang.
17. would be, lent.
18. has improved, stayed.
19. have you not drunk, was ordered.
20. worked, would fail.

Exercise 20 :

1. was walking, met, said, had forgotten, was, would be, writes, is writing, hoping.

2. have not seen, came.
3. fignts, is honoured.
4. was lying, managed.
5. gave, had finished.
6. was studying, heard, shouting, went, was, was, had come, tried, told, had rung, should have gone, opened.
7. did not make, would not be punished.
8. was walking, saw, was sitting, begging.
9. was returning, saw, lying, was attacked, ran.
10. would not have seen.
11. was looking, saw, walking, are you going, have not seen, left.
12. rains, shall be, agree, may spend, rowing, have not spent, was saved, drowning, had fallen, shall be, go, should fall.

Exercise 21:-

1. The prince **was given** nice food by the old woman..
2. They **will be conquered** by us.
3. The money **has been stolen** by the thief.
4. **Meat is eaten** by some people for breakfast.
5. Football **was played** well by him.
6. The watch **was lost** by the girl.
7. A cake **is eaten** by me every day.
8. Some words have **been written** by him.
9. A book **was being bought** by her.
10. My brother **was taught** English by me.

Exercise 22:-

1. Some eggs were bought by him from the farmer.
2. Sometimes a small army wins a great battle.
3. A bear was killed by him.

4. A present was given to the boy by him.
5. Corn is ground by the miller into flour.
6. An obelisk was being cut by the stone cutters of a great mass of rock.
7. My orders have always been obeyed by him.
8. Many towns have been left by the last war in ruins.
9. I was deceived by his trick.
10. The lessons are read by the teachers.

Exercise 23:

1. Food is cooked by her.
2. My friend was visited by me.
3. Football will be played by us.
4. Questions are being answered by them.
5. Fruit has been eaten by him.
6. Many bombs were dropped by the aeroplanes on the town.
7. The ceilling cannot be reached by us.
8. Illness is caused by dirt.
9. The child is being examined by the doctor.
10. How to read the ancient writings was discovered by the learned men.
11. The enemy will be conquered by a strong army.
12. Some nails were knocked by the carpenter into the chair.
13. The books are arranged nicely by a tidy boy in his desk.
14. Sailing ships are driven by the wind over the water.
15. The thief was caught by the policeman although he ran fast.

Exercise 24:-

1. Germs **can be seen** by you. **C**an germs be seen by you?

2.   This story **was told** to you **by whom. By whom was** this story told to you?

3.   The story of the prisoner **has been heard** by you. **Has the** story of the prisoner been heard by you ?

4.   These boys **are often met** by you. **Are** these boys often met by you?

5.   The window **was broken by whom. By whom was** the window broken?

6.   The book **be** shut. **Let** the book be shut.

7.   The flowers **are watered by** the gardener. **Are** the flowers watered by the gardener?

8.   The lesson **be** read. **Let** the lesson be read.

9.   My fountain-pen **has been seen** by anybody. **Has my fountain-pen** been seen by anybody?

10. The books **have been borrowed** by whom. **By whom** have the books been borrowed?

Exercise 25:-

1.   The books **are taken** care of by Nadia.

2.   The baby **has been** dressed by her.

3.   The lesson **was** explained by the teacher.

4.   A house **will be** bought by Zaki.

5.   Our lessons **must be** studied by us.

6.   A letter **may be** written by him.

7.   A noise **is being** made by Nagi.

8.   The hut **was being** guarded by the dog.

9.   The bird **had been** killed by Hoda.

10. **By whom was** the milk drunk?

11. **Why will** flies be killed by us ?

12. **When shall I be** visited by you?

13. **By whom was** the window broken?

14. **Who was** visited by them?

15. **By whom was** the exercise written?

Exercise 26:-

a) A heavy load was being carried by the camel.
b) Many presents have been given by her to her sisters
c) A string will be wound by me round my finger.
d) Because he was angry, some insulting words were said by him.
e) The university was left by him although he was clever.

Exercise 27:-

1. Two questions have been asked by her to me.
2. Their father has been seen by the boys.
3. The market will be shown by me to you.
4. The two appels were not eaten by him.
5. The lazy boys have been punished by the teacher.
6. They have been told a nice story by him.
7. Cotton, wheat and maize are grown by farmes in Egypt.
8. The city could not be defended by the army.
9. A car is bought by a merchant for L.E. 500.
10. The cart is being pulled by the donkey along the street.
11. All his possessions have been sold by him.
12. Was the bell rung by the servant?
13. Let a letter be written to your father.
14. Strong drink had been taken by him.
15. Was the tree being cut down by the men?

Exercise 28:-

1. The policeman catches the thief.
2. A motor-car ran over the child.

3. Who broke the mirror?
4. Does the gardener water the flowers?
5. The employer is not paying the workmen.
6. She can write a letter.
7. Ali has found the book.
8. Who beat him?
9. The boy beats the cat.
10. He was ringing the bell.
11. They are selling bread.
12. Shut the door.
13. The baby will eat the food.
14. The cat catches the mice.
15. The wind shook the branches.

Exercise 29:-

1. Did not play.
2. Does not cook.
3. Does not drink.
4. Shall not go.
5. Do not pay.
6. Cannot sweep.
7. Does not guard.
8. Do not come.
9. is not running.
10. Did not buy.

Exercise 30:-

1. You have **not** seen this picture **either.**
2. My brother never helps me.
3. No boy received a prize.
4. He **does not** run **so** quickly as his brother.
5. The servant **did not** lose ten piastres yesterday, **neither** did I.

6. He **never** wastes his time.
7. I met **neither** Ali **nor** Ahmed.
8. **Nobody** is waiting for us.
9. **Not all** the servants are honest.
10. He forgot **neither** his book **nor** his pen.

Exercise 31:-

1. I have not been in Alexandria either.
2. You can obtain no money in this way.
3. Nobody is playing in the garden.
4. On the moon, there is not water either.
5. This man is neither a robber nor a beggar.
6. None of them can sing.
7. He ought not to do so.
8. Animals know not all these things.
9. He never writes with a pencil.
10. Neither he nor his friend **is** in France.
11. There are germs nowhere or, there are not germs anywhere.
12. They never visit us.
13. He never comes late.
14. He never eats much fruit.
15. Not all the pupils were at school.
16. Hassan has not a car either.
17. He did not do his work either.
18. I shall tell nobody what you are doing.
19. He will have neither the book nor the pen.
20. I bought no books, or I did not buy any books.

Exercise 32:-

1. **Who** killed a bear?
2. **Who** have books?
3. **Who** saw a bird?

4. **Who** go to school?
5. **What** ran after the mice?
6. **What** gives us milk?
7. **What** rises in summer?
8. **What** could answer questions?
9. **Whom** did she see in the street?
10. **Whom** did the king marry?
11. **Whom** will he meet to-morrow?
12. **Whom** does the boy thank?
13. **What** did he see?
14. **What** has a man?
15. **What** did he shoot?
16. **What** does Ali drink?
17. **Where** did he put his handkerchief?
18. **Where** were we looking?
19. **Where** did the dwarfs stay?
20. **Where** did he go?
21. **Whose** house is this?
22. **Whose** leg was broken?
23. **Whose** bag was lost?
24. **Whose** brother did you meet?
25. **Why** did he go home?
26. **Why** does a horse go to the river?
27. **Why** do we come to school?
28. **Why** was the child weeping?
29. **When** will he come?
30. **When** do they get up?
31. **When** does he go to the cinema?
32. **When** do they come to school?

Exercise 33:-

1. **How** did the old man walk?
2. **How** did he shoot the rabbit?

3. **How** did she look?
4. **How** does he go to school?
5. **How tall** is Zaki?
6. **How far** is it from Cairo to the Pyramids?
7. **How many** passengers does a bus carry?
8. **How much** will you pay for this book?
9. **How** can people travel from Cairo to Alex.?
10. **How high is** this wall?
11. **How many** hands have you?
12. **How many** windows has the room?
13. **How many** boys are there in the class-room?
14. **How old** is he?

Exercise 34:-

1. Where.
2. How many.
3. Whom.
4. Who.
5. Where.
6. How far.
7. When.
8. What.
9. Whose.
10. How high.

Exercise 35:-

1. **How** does he come to school?
2. **Where** does the river Nile begin?
3. **How** are houses built?
4. **Where** is your house?
5. **When** is the Nile in flood?
6. **How much** did you pay for the bag?
7. **How far** is it from Cairo to Helwan?

8. **How many** pupils passed in the examination?
9. **How** does the train travel?
10. **Why** was he punished?
11. **How much** did you pay for your English book?
12. **When** does the bell ring?
13. **Why** was he rewarded?
14. **Why** cannot you hold the pot?
15. **Where** do we see plays?
16. **What** would you do if you were urgent?
17. **How** does he come to school?
18. **Why** did you come late?
19. **Why** did you visit him?
20. **How fast** can an aeroplane travel?
21. **When** did the band stop playing?
22. **Where** will a new city be built?
23. **How many** months are there in a year?
24. **Is** your father at home?
25. **When** will they visit us?

Exercise 36:-

1. At last he said **that he could** not go on any more and that he had never been so hungry in his life.

2. The teacher always **says** that that is the **worst** class he had met till then.

3. The teacher said that that boy had been absent during the accident and that he hoped that everything would be clear by the next day.

4. They said that they had found that coat. **Jacob said that** it was his son's coat.

5. He said that he had no money with him then, but he would give him some money the next day.

6. Everyone shouted that he was drowning and could

not swim.

7. He said that he could not return that day or the next day.

8. The man **says** that he is a guilty man and **deserves** punishment.

9. I told Ali that he could go the next day.

10. The criminal said that he was going to confess and added that he had robbed the man of his money and had given it to his brother.

12. The lady said that she could not pay that high price.

13. The man said that he was going away a week from that day.

14. The boy said that he had found that book. Ali said that it was his book.

15. **The boy told his father** that he had promised to tell him a story.

16. **The man said** that he was glad that he was going to Egypt.

17. My friend told me that the day before he had found my book under his desk.

Exercise 37:-

a) He said, « I shall come as soon as I can ».

b) The station master said to me, «The train has gone. There is not another train until to-morrow».

c) He said to me, «You may leave this place as soon as you can».

d) Ali said, «I should be top of the class, if I was not not prevented by illness from attending school then.»

e) He wrote to me saying, «I shall expect you to arrive to-morrow.»

f) She said, «I have never seen so many beautiful flowers.»

g) The boy said, «I shall go for a ride on my bicycle.»

h) Patruchio said to her father, «I love her more than ever. I have prepared everything for our marriage to-morrow».

i) The officer said to himself, «The knight can beat the bravest of our warriors».

j) The boy said to his father, «I have succeded. I want a bicycle as a reward».

k) He said, «I feel sure that there is some fearful quarrel in the room».

l) They said, «We have not heard of a more exciting event before».

m) He said, «I am not interested in other people's matters.»

n) They said to us, «We promise to pay the money to-morrow».

Exercise 38:-

1. I asked Aly to whom he had given my book the night before.

2. He asks the policeman which way leads to the station.

3. He asked me what time it was and if I was coming then.

4. I shall say to Nabil if he is sure he will come.

5. I asked my brother if he did not remember that

when he had gone away he had taken his book away.

6. The doctor asked the sick man if he would have liked to take that drug.

7. I asked him if **he had been** absent the day before.

8. The teacher asked the new pupil what his name was and how old he was.

9. The soldier asked the swallow if he would not stay with him for one night and be his messenger **and added that** the boy might die of thirst and the mother might die of grief.

10. The headmaster asked who had been absent the day before.

11. My brother asked if I could lend him a piastre.

12. I asked my servant if my shoes had been cleaned.

13. The father asked his son what he wanted then.

14. He asked in anger why he was so late and where he had been.

15. The tailor asked me if I wanted a woollen suit.

16. The teacher asked who had been absent there the day before.

17. My mother asked the servant if he had broken these plates.

18. I asked the butcher's son what he was doing with that knife and if he wanted to kill us.

19. Ali asked me if I should go to Alex. that summer.

20. The policeman asked the driver what the number of his car was and why he drove so fast.

Exercise 39:-

1. I said to Ali, «Is it necessary to dip a fountain-pen in the ink?».

2. I said to the gardener, «What do you know about

the old man? Who is he?».

3. Mohamed said to his sister, «Don't you think this is a good idea?».

4. The sick man said to the doctor, «Is it necessary for me to keep in bed all time?»

5. My father said to me, «Have you done your home-work for to-morrow? Are your teachers satisfied with you?».

6. He said to me, «How old are you? What is your address?».

7. The judge said to him, «By whom have you been robbed? How much have you lost?».

8. I said to him, «Who helped you? When have you arrived? Where are you going to-morrow?».

9. The boy said to his father, «I have succeeded. When will you buy me the watch?».

10. The boy scout said to the tourist, «I shall take you to wherever you wish to go, as I am free this morning». The tourist replied, «You are very kind. If you can direct me to the station, all will be well, as I have a train to catch in ten minutes from now.»

Exercise 40:-

1. He begged me to lend him some money.

2. The teacher advised the pupil to write his name clearly.

3. The master ordered the servant to go at once and to bring him a pen with which be could write.

4. Ali told Zaki to let him ride his bicycle for half an hour.

5. The judge ordered the policeman to take him back to prison and not to let him escape again.

6. The child begged not to leave him alone.

7. The beggar begged me to give him a piastre **and** said **that he was weak.**

8. The prisoner **told** the judge **that** he was innocent and **begged him** to take pity on his poor children.

9. Ali begged him to look for him because his father was there.

10. I begged my father to excuse the mistake I had made.

11. Fahmi **told Ali** to come to his house and to see him that afternoon.

12. The father ordered his son to leave him alone and to tell his mother that he was busy.

13. The wounded man begged me to give him some water and said that he was dying of thirst.

14. The doctor told my friend that he was ill and advised him to go bed and added that he would come to see him the next day.

15. He requested his guest to stay for the party.

16. Ali's father ordered him to work hard and told him that he would give him five pounds if he passed his examination.

17. The officer ordered him to tell him his name or he would send him to prison.

18. The policeman ordered him to stop and that he could not go any further.

19. He ordered his son not to play with that thing when he was speaking to him.

20. Ahmed told Mohamed not to leave him then and asked why he wanted to go when he had been there for only a minute.

Exercise 41:-

1. The pupils shouted with joy that their team had won the match.

2. The porter said with anger that that bag was heavy.

3. The father said with sorrow that there was no hope in his recovery.

4. He told me with admiration that my garden was beautiful.

5. The pupil cried with joy that he had passed his examination.

6. He shouted with sorrow that he had made a mistake.

7. The beggar said with sadness that he was dying of hunger.

8. The Egyptians said with victory that they had defeated the British, French and Israeli armies in Port-Said.

9. The Egyptian pilot said with victory that he had destroyed the enemy's harbour.

10. I told my friend with admiration that his clothes were fine.

Exercise 42:-

1. He told me that he would visit me the next day.

2. He asked the policeman if he had caught the thief the day before.

3. The man told the owner of the house that he would rent the flat and asked how much he would charge him.

4. The little girl asked her mother where she could find her book. The mother answered that she did not know and advised her to look for it in her room because she had seen it there the day before.

5. Ali asked Hassan if he had seen his brother that day.

6. Hassan said that he had seen him the day before.
7. I told my brother that I thought that he might come soon.
8. Ali thanked him very much.
9. Petruchio told himself (thought) that he would tame her and teach her to obey and that he could see an improvement already.
10. Pyecraft told me that he had tried western drugs and asked if I could give him a bit of my grandmother's stuff and that it might reduce his weight.
11. The father told his son that that was his room.
12. Sami said that he would fly to Italy the next day.
13. Tom is asking me if I am ill.
14. His friend asked him if he liked to be with them and added that they were going to visit the market
15. The father asked the boy why he had not gone to his uncle as he told him and added that he deserved severe beating and ordered him to go then and to bring the books in that bag.
16. The doctor asked me how I had broken my arm.
17. The boy asked the teacher if he might go home then and added that he had finished all he had got to do that day.
18. The teacher ordered him to put his books away but not to be late the next day as he would have an examination.
19. He asked Ali if he was coming there the next day to talk about that matter.
20. My father often asks me if I am working hard.
21. Tom asked me if I had been ill the day before.
22. The man told me that he had not a job for two months and he had a wife and family to keep and asked if I could give him some work and that he

was a carpenter. I replied that I had nothing to give him that day but if he could come the next day I should find him some. He thanked me and said that he would certainly be there the next morning.

23. He said that he felt ill and asked if he might go home and added that he could not do any more work.

24. Mr. Smith asked the applicant how fast he could type. The applicant replied that he could type eighty words a minute. Mr. Smith ordered to let him see his letters of recommendation and added that he wanted the copies only and he might keep the originals.

25. The servant said that he would send the letter at once.

Exercise 43 : -

1. He told the boys that they would hardly reach the falls that night at that rate and ordered them to make haste and not to waste their time.

2. He told his friend that he would come there the next day.

3. He ordered the boys to come along up on deck and that he would keep them under guard.

4. The doctor asked the girl why she had not come to see him the day before and that she was very feverish then.

5. The headmaster asked the boy why he had been late the day before and if he could never come early and added that if he was late the next day he would be dismissed.

6. Sami advised Ali not to drive too fast and added that they were not in a great hurry.

7. A foreign voice asked what he was doing there.

8. Ali greeted his friend in the morning and asked him where he was going then and added that he wanted to go with him to the cinema.

9 His father said if he went abroad he would be the most miserable boy that ever had been born and tnat he could give no consent to it.

10. I told the pupils that I was glad to meet them both

11. Ali asked if he thought he was quite honest.

12. I begged Ali to go and call a doctor then.

13. The boy begged his father to take him to the circus.

14. The friend has often asked when he is coming to see him.

15. The teacher asked his pupils if they had been to the zoo.

16. The judge asked if he would confess **that he was** guilty.
The prisoner said that he would not, as he was not guilty.
The judge asked if he knew the criminal. **The prisoner said** that he might ask the police.

17. He asked me if I liked eating the meat of pigs and added that a man who ate that kind **of meat would look like** a pig.

18. The shopkeeper said that he had no fruit that day and asked if he could offer him anything else and added that his tinned fruit was fresh.

19. **The merchant ordered the builder** to build him a house like that of a prince and not to forget to surround it with a garden and added that in six months he hoped to occupy it.

20. The traveller asked the guide if there was anyone

there who spoke French and added that he did not **know** any other language.

21. The small boy asked why the Japanese built their houses of paper. **His father said** that there were earthquakes in Japan. **The small boy asked** when the houses fell down, what they did. **His father said** that they carried them off to another place.

22. When we had finished, he said that there would be no more work until the next day, and ordered to bring his tools with him and to be ready to start at seven o'clock.

23. **His father said** that he had heard of his success, but not to forget that life contained more than what was contained in books.

24. She asked what that meant and if he had brought her bad news. He replied that he had left their army advancing against the enemy the night before and added that their army was then winning the battle.

25. The officer asked if he had got them. **Tai sang replied that** they were in the cellar under his shop.

26. **The speaker asked** if they were to believe his words and added that he had often told them lies and advised to let him prove his statements.

27. The mother asked the child if he knew **that it was** nearly nine o'clock and added that it **was time he** had been in bed.

28. Nemo asked Ali if he was interested in machinery. Ali **agreed and said that** he was being trained in the motor-car works. Nemo told him to come and **see his motor-car.**

Exercise 44 : -

1. **Orlando told Oliver** that he had his consent and that he could have his wedding the next day and that he would invite the duke as well as his fri - ends and **ordered him** to go to persuade his lady **and added that** she was then alone.

2. The policeman asked what he was doing there . The stranger replied that was not his business. The policeman said that it would soon be his busi- ness if he loitered much longer outside that jewe- ller's shop after it was closed and added that he had better move on.

3. Sir Henry smiled as he told **lad** that the hour was late for a philosophical discussion and that he had letters to write and that it was a fine night then and ordered to leave him alone for a while and asked why he would not go for a short walk.

4. She asked me if I should rather ride my own bi- cycle or borrow hers. I replied that if she did not mind I should rather ride my own.

5. Mr. Justice Pantin asked what he wanted. The stranger replied that he wanted to talk to him. The judge said that he did not think he knew him and asked who he was. The man said that he dou- bted whether his name would mean anything to him because at the moment it was Smith.

Exercise 45 : -

1. The boys shouted, «Hurrah! We have won the game».

2. My brother said, « Alas! It is a long time since you have seen me».

3. The engineer said to the workman, «**What are you doing?**» The latter answered, «I had nothing to do for three hours». Then engineer said to him. «Follow what I myself am busy repairing».

4. The judge said to him, «By whom were you robbed? How much did you lose?»

5. I said to him, « Who helped you? When have you arrived? Where are you going to-morrow?»

6 I said to him, «Do your duty».

7. We said to him, «Do not walk through the wood **to-night**».

8. The beggar said to the passer-by, «Please, give me a piastre».

9. The teacher said to the pupil, «Do your work carefully because you will lose marks for carelessness». The pupil answered , «I am ready to do my best».

10. The man said to his son, «Go to bed early, because we are going to Cairo to-morrow».

11. The teacher said to the pupil,«**Do** not be in a hurry. **If** you do, you will be sorry.»

12. Tom said to Mary, «I have never been to the circus. Will you like to go there with me to-morrow.»

Exercise 46 : -

1. I saw a boy **who** was sitting on the chair.

2. There are hunters **who live near the forest** in this town.

3. The servants **who thought that there was a ghost** in the house were afraid.

4. This is the fisherman **who** catches fish from the river.

5. The boy **who was ill** went to the doctor.

6. Sami caught a thief **who** was in the house.

7. Merchants **who sold goods** went from town to town.
8. Here is Mary **who** cooks well.
9. Every boy **who learns his lessons** has a chance of success.
10. The man **who had an axe** cut down the tree.
11. Three men **who found a purse** were travelling together.
12. The doctor came to see the man **who was** ill.
13. The policeman arrested the thief **who** was leaving the shop.
14. Where is Mary **who** is playing tennis ?
15. I met the man **who** is your brother.
16. You met Zaki **who** was crossing the street.
17. This is the boy **who** stole my watch.
18. The man **who is an Egyptian** is teaching us English.
19. Do you know the teacher **who** wrote this book ?
20. My sister **who is interested in reading** is reading a book.

Exercise 47 :-

1. The boy **whom you saw** is my brother.
2. I saw the man **for whom we were waiting.**
3. The boy **whom we met in the garden** had a nice dog.
4. Did you see the man **about whom I had spoken to you** ?
5. There are many pupils **whom we know** in the school.
6. Did you meet the merchant **from whom you bought** a motor-car ?

7. My brother **for whom his friend is waiting** is not in the house.

8. Amin **whom you know** is my uncle.

9. Here is the pupil **from whom the teacher is angry.**

10. I respect the honest man **with whom you work.**

11. A child **whom we found** was lost in the city.

12. The boy **whom the doctor ordered to stay in bed** was ill.

13. Ali **whom I met in the barrage** was riding a donkey.

14. He is the leader **on whom we can depend.**

15. A beggar **to whom she was kind** came to her door.

Exercise 48 :-

1. The ox **which the butcher killed** was very fat.

2. You must not eat the fruit **which is unripe.**

3. Mary ate the cake **which you gave her.**

4. He told us a story **which was funny.**

5. Our kitchen **in which we prepare the food** is clean

6. They are in the sitting room **in which there are beautiful pictures.**

7. He gave me a **watch for which I thanked him.**

8. The exercise **which you asked me to do** was easy.

9. The fountain pen **with which I am writing** is good.

10. This is the book **about which** you told me.

11. This is the window **which** he broke.

12. Did you send the letter **which I told you to write** ?

13. This is a very difficult exercise **which no one can answer.**

14. Tell me your address **which is new.**

15. The broken sword **which we shall throw away** does not melt.

Exercise 49 :-

1. I met Ali **whose bag was lost.**
2. I know the man **whose brother is an officer.**
3. Here is the boy **whose father is my friend.**
4. The farmer **whose dog died** was sad.
5. My teacher **with whose help I succeed** is good.
6. The jeweller **from whose shop the thieves stole jewels** became poor.
7. This is the boy **whose pen I borrowed.**
8. The men **whose clothes are made of wool** feel warm.
9. The policeman caught the thief **whose leg was broken.**
10. We comforted the boy **whose brother died.**
11. I saw a soldier **whose arm was cut off.**
12. **Ali whose finger was cut with a knife felt pain.**
13. The lady **in whose house Mary lives** is very kind.
14. Yesterday I visited Maged **whose brother came from Alex.**
15. The boy **from whose desk a book has been stolen** is very annoyed.

Exercise 50 :-

1. The tree **which stood in the middle of the street** was cut down.
2. That village **in which I was born** is very small.
3. The boy **who jumped out of the window** broke his arm.
4. The man **at whose house we stayed** is my uncle.
5. My father has bought a motor-car **for which he has paid L.E. 500.**
6. I saw a dog **which was carrying a bone.**

7. I met a beautiful girl **who had golden hair.**
8. I know the man **whose son is a doctor.**
9. Did you see the girl **about whom I had spoken to you ?**
10. The marks **which were put on the candles** showed the hours.
11. Many of the men **who came to the Nile Valley** were able to find food.
12. Every year there was a great flood **which brought life to all plants.**
13. The sheep **from whose back wool came** is living quite happily in some distant country.
14. The farmer **whose donkey we have hired** is in the field.
15. Have you met the man **whose son you teach ?**
16. Here are the books **for which you are looking.**
17. He has an overcoat **which protects him from cold.**
18. Rustum built a splendid palace **to which he retired to spend the rest of his life.**
19. She sent a present to her daughter **whom she loved dearly.**
20. We tried to comfort the woman **whose eyes were full of tears.**

Exercise 51 :-

1. **Although** he is rich, he is unhappy.
2. **Although** Mary works hard, she fails.
3. **Although** the river is wide, I can cross it.
4. He was given a prize **although he did not win the match.**
5. **Although** there was a war, Egyptians were not frightened.
6. **Although** it was raining, he went out.

7. **Although** a metal shines it is not real gold.
8. He was very hungry **although** he ate a good meal.
9. **Although** Karam learnt his lesson, he did not remember it.
10. **Although** the rich man has a motor car, he never rides it.

Exercise 52 :-

1. The child wept **because** his mother beat him.
2. Mary bought a piece of cloth **because** she wanted to make a new dress.
3. Karam caught the train **because** he came early.
4. **Because** the pupil made a noise, the teacher punished him.
5. I found none **because** they all had gone on a visit.
6. **Because** Samy was ill, he stayed at home.
7. I thanked the teacher **because** he gave me a reward.
8. Amin complained of Nagi because he hit him with a stick.
9. We drink because we are thirsty.
10. You can go now **because** your teacher has given you permission.

Exercise 53:-

1. **While** the boy was running, he fell down.
2. He lay in bed **after** he had reached home.
3. It rained while **I** was returning home.
4 **As soon as** the mother reached home, her children ran to meet her.
5. **When** the man arrived, his friend welcomed him.
6. Nobody knows **when** the train will arrive.
7. **After** he **had come** to school, he entered the class.

8. **While** Zaki **was driving** his car, he ran over a child.
9. I know the time **when** my friend will come.
10. Nagi ate the cake **after he had bought it.**

Exercise 54:-

1. You will be rich **if** you work hard.
2. **If** I visit him, he will be pleased.
3. They would win the match **if** they played well.
4. **If** Kamel eats much, he will be fat.
5. We shall not play football **if** it rains.

Exercise 55:-

1. I don't like Fred **because** he is dishonest.
2. He has never been to college **although** he is **very** clever.
3. He works hard **because** he likes to succeed.
4. **Although** he found his watch, he lost it again.
5. He jumped into the river **because** he wanted to swim to the other bank.
6. **As soon as (When)** we heard the bell, we entered the classroom.
7. He put on a heavy coat **because** it was very cold.
8. He went to Cairo to visit his friend whom he had not seen for two years.
9. He was hurt **because** he fell off his horse.
10. It wish **that** the fan would work.
11. The roots are crushed **because** we want to make medicines.
12. **Because** her generosity was very great, she helped everybody who asked for help. **OR** She **whose generoisty was very great** helped everybody who asked for help.

13. **Because** the blow was very strong, the knight sank to the ground.
14. The man committed the robbery **although** he pretented that he had not.
15. The man pretented to be blind **because** he wished to get money easily.
16. I heard a loud noise **while** I was studying my lessons.
17. Although Fatma was careless, she succeeded **because** she was lucky.
18. **Although** he shouted many times, no one heard him.
19. I feel tired **because** I have worked hard.
20. **Because** Samy lives all alone, he is always glad to have a visitor.
21. **Although** he ran very fast, he missed the train.
22. I feel tired **although** I have not worked hard.
23. **Although** he fought bravely, he was defeated.
24. The bell rang **after we had gone** to our classroom.
25. She answered my question **although** the question was very difficult.

Exercise 56 : -

1. Ahmed went home **after** he had finished his **work although** it was difficult **(OR which was difficult).**
2. **When** the train arrived at the station, I met my friend **whom** I have not seen for two weeks.
3. **While** the lady was shouting, the thief ran away after he had stolen her bag.
4. **When** the doctor examined him, he ordered him to stay in bed.
5. He was forced to stay in the house because(while) it was raining.

6. **Although** Aly's father gave him three pounds every month, he was always in debt **because he** was very wasteful with his money.

7. **Because** their motor-car broke down ten miles from the nearest village, the passengers continued on foot where they arrived at sunset.

8. Ali tried to sell his motor-car to Mohamed **who** refused to buy it **because** he said that it was too expensive.

9. Watches **which are made in Switzerland** are the best in the world **because** they keep perfect time.

10. **As soon as** Mohamed finished his breakfast, he hurried to the station **because** he wanted to catch the twelve o'clock train.

11. The workman was repairing the telegraph wire which was broken because the wind blew very severely the day before yesterday.

12. I could not come and see you **because** the roads were very muddy **after** it had rained very hard yesterday.

13. I expect to go to England **if I** succeed in the examination **which will be held next year.**

14. **Although** Napoleon was a great general, he was conquered in the end **while he was fighting** against the rest of Europe.

15. **As soon as** the man was hurt in a street accident, he was sent to hospital **in which** he recovered from his hurts.

Exercise 57 : -

1. The **broken cup beyond repair** lay in shining pieces on the floor.

2. He took his spoon **to eat. OR Taking his spoon,** he began to eat.

3. Join these sentences **without using and or but. OR** Don't use and or but **in joining these sentences.**

4. **Having been disobedient you** cannot come with us to the barrage. **OR** You cannot come with us to the barrage **for being disobedient.**

5. **On reading the report,** I found that he had been killed in a railway accident.

6. The very numerous insects covered the field with their bodies. **OR Being very numerous,** the insects covered the field with their bodies.

7. **On finishing her breakfast,** Mary hurried to the station **to catch the train.**

8. **Getting up early,** Ali came to school slowly.

9. **Finishing his difficult work,** Karam went home.

10. I saw Sami **coming to school** on a rainy day.

Exercise 58 : -

1. Not only **did** he speak clearly **but also** he told the truth.

2. Some people can **neither** read **nor** write.

3. The man was a thief **but** he was innocent.

4. **Not only** did he break his promise **but also** he told a lie.

5. **Not only** can he drive a motor-car **but also** he can ride a horse.

6. There is **neither** ink nor there is chalk in the class-room .

7. Either the door was left open or it was opened from outside.

8. Mary is **not only** clever **but also** she is a hard worker.
9. **Not only are** cotton clothes pretty **but also** they are cheap.
10. There was a storm **but** the ship was saved.
11. He likes apples **and** he is fond of oranges.
12. **Either** he pays the debt **or** he will be put in prison.
13. **Neither** are those boys clever **nor** they are careful.
14. **Either** your friend is a doctor **or** he is a teacher.
15. Ali went home **and** lay in bed.
16. The thief was caught **and** was put prison.
17. **Either** you must work hard or your father will be angry with you.
18. Our army was small **but** he conquered the **English** army .
10. Neither can she cook nor she can wash.
20. **Not only** was Mary kind to the beggar **but also** she gave him clothes.

Exercise 59: -

1. Tell me where you live.
2. He refused to carry out what I commanded.
3. We must hope that you will succeed.
4. We know who makes the chair.
5. He did not hear that his father died.
6. He died when he was sixty years old.
7. He was afraid that he would fail.
8. I met who built the house.
9. Write down how old you are.
10. None knew how much she weighed.
11. Mary told me that she had married.
12. I congratulated him on what he spoke.
13. Can you tell me how high the pyramid is.

14. She knows how she can make sweets.
15. Do you know how much this shoe costs.
16. Karam forgot where he was born.
17. None knows why he is absent.
18. A father buys what his son wants.
19. No one knows how deep the sea is.
20. I heard that he arrived to Cairo.

Exercise 60 : -

1. Bring **your necessities** with you.
2. Do not forget **the place** of your examination.
3. My father knows the **width** of this room.
4. He did not tell me **the reason for** his coming.
5. Mary knows **the meaning** of this word.
6. I was glad to hear **of his success.**
7. Do you know **the distance** between the earth and the moon.
8. We agreed to his speech.
9. Ali told me **the price** of this book.
10. Tell the teacher **the number** of the boys in **the** class.
11. The mother knows **the reason** of her child's weeping.
12. The applicant wrote down **his address.**
13. Huda knows **the way** to make cakes.
14. Every woman lies about **her age.**
15. **His description to the battle** was right.

Exercise 61 : -

1. The boat **which is on the river** has no sail.
2. Stones **which are lying on the road** are dangerous.
3. Every boy **who is in this class** must work hard.

4. The train **which will go to Alexandria** will leave at four o'clock.
5. The goods **which were in the shop window** were damaged by fire.
6. The petrol **which is found in Egypt** is large in quantity.
7. I like to have a house **which is surrounded with a garden.**
8. The woman **who is carrying a basket** sells oranges.
9. The girl **who is clever** succeeds every day.
10. A dog **which was mad** bit my brother **who was little.**
11. In winter we put on clothes **which are made of wool.**
12. The soldier **who is with one arm** cannot fight well.
13. Mary has a garden full of flowers **which are beautiful.**
14. I admire **who writes this book.**
15. We believe the man **who is honest.**
16. The man **who was dead** was burried in grave.
17. The men **who were brave** defended Egypt.
18. Samy wrote a story **which** was interesting.
19. The passengers **who were in the train** were injured in the accident.
20. A boy **who is clever** must depend on himself in answering a question **which is difficult.**

Exercise 62 : -

1. **A poor man** has no food.
2. The **clever** boy answers the **difficult** exercise.
3. **Beautiful** birds build nests of straw.
4. The **careless** girl did not write the exercise.
5. I have an **honest** servant.

6. Karam bought a book **with a red cover.**
7. Mary puts on **silk** clothes.
8. The **little** boy cannot join the army.
9. The **brave** soldier shot the aeroplane.
10. Fatma cooks **sweet** food.

Exercise 63 : -

1. The police **should** catch him.
2. They **may** read them.
3. The pupils might understand.
4. We **may** learn.
5. He **may** succeed.
6. He **might** be rich.
7. The school **should** dismiss him.
8. He **should** give you less money.
9. She **might** go to school early.
10. He **might** eat food.
11. They **may** protect themselves against the sun.
12. I **might** laugh.
13. The child **should** be hurt.
14. They **might** talk with me.
15. They **may** read books.

Exercise 64 : -

1. We went to Alex. **in order to (to, so as to)** enjoy fresh air.
2. He works hard **so as to** succeed.
3. He took his spoon **in order that (so that, that) he might eat.**
4. We went to the garden **so that we might breathe fresh air.**

5. They worked hard **lest they should fail.**
6. Karam went to the cinema **in order that he might** see the film.
7. We go to school **so that we may** learn.
8. He bought a fountain pen **in order that he might** write with it.
9. Certain drugs are used **so that they may** kill the cotton worm.
10. He went to his house **to** meet us.
11. She sleeps early **so as not to** be late.
12. We all **work in order to eat.**
13. The teacher watched the pupils very carefully for fear of the cheating of someone.
14. Do your duty **so as not to** be punished.
15. Boys play football **in order that they may be** strong.

Exercise 65 : -

1. I could not see the way.
2. The porter cannot carry it.
3. Is he that he cannot succeed.
4. That he wins the match.
5. He could not move.
6. Everyone understood him.
7. He was punished.
8. Everyone loved him.
9. That he could not work.
10. That she got high marks.
11. He cannot **come.**
12. That the **teacher became angry with him.**
13. Of his success that I shouted.
14. We stayed at **home.**
15. He fell senseless.

Exercise 66 :

1.   Tom is **so ill that** he cannot go to school.
2.   Mary was **so clever that** she could not make silly mistakes.
3.   The boy was **too frightened** to move.
4.   She is good **enough for everyone to** praise her.
5   He was **so weak that** he could not swim any more.
6.   I was **so tired that** I could not go with him.
7.   The baby is **so young that** he cannot walk.
8.   The time was **too short for us to** answer the exercise.
9.   Ali is **too poor to buy** food.
10. The bag was **too heavy for the porter to** carry it.

Exercise 67 :

1.   They were easy.
2.   You will get high marks.
3.   He came.
4.   You will make mistakes.
5.   He made the same mistake.
6.   He is, he will not buy a motor-car.
7.   You will be punished.
8.   The thief ran away.
9.   He made many mistakes.
10. We shall conquer them.
11. They are dirty.
12. Letters you may send him.
13. He is not afraid of darkness.
14. He was afraid of the dog.
15. He did not behave well.

Exercise 68:-

1. **Although she talked much** she has done nothing.
2. I believe you **in spite of telling lies.**
3. He will always be miserable **in spite of earning money.**
4. **Although he ran quickly,** he could not catch the thief.
5. **Although we came by taxi,** we came late.
6. **Althongh he was lazy** he passed the examination.
7. **Although he was poor** he was happy.
8. **Although he worked hard** he failed.
9. **In spite of his loud voice, I** heard nothing.
10. **For all his reading,** he understands nothing.
11. **Although it is cold, I** feel quite warm.
12. **He defeated that champion although he was small in size.**
13. The prisoner **escaped whatever precautions the police made.**
14. He has little to show **although he works hard.**
15. **Although I advised him,** he continued to make mistakes.

Exercise 69:-

1. He had no shoes.
2. It was broken.
3. He lost the match.
4. They carry germs.
5. He did not know the solution of the matter.

Exercise 70:-

1. **Because of being young,** he did not join the army.
2. He stayed at home **because of his illness.**

3. Mary studies her lessons easily **because of being clever.**

4. He was able to buy a motor-car **because of being rich.**

5. I admire this King **owing to his kindness to his subjects.**

6. I like this boy **because (as, since, for) he respects his parents.**

7. I dislike this man **because he is ill-humoured.**

8. This boy failed in the examination **because ,(as since, for) he was careless.**

9. This boy succeeded **because (as, since, for)** he was clever.

10. I am safe **because of your help.**

11. **Because the teacher was severe,** the class sat silent.

12. **Because he was foolish** many people were injured.

13. **Because the doctor was skillfull,** the man's life was saved.

14. The boats could not cross the river **because of fearfulness of the flood.**

15. The swimmer could not cross the river **because of the rapidness of the current.**

Exercise 71:-

1. The singer finished.

2. I order you.

3. I have not seen him.

4. He fell down.

5. I received my friend.

6. Her child was ill.

7. Have grown much cotton.

8. Than he ran away.

9. Than he went to school.

10. It rained.
11. He knocked him down.
12. He saw a thief.
13. He fell down.
14. He went to the classroom.
15. Than he caught many fish.

Exercise 72:-

1. **While I was walking** in the street, I met Mary.
2. **Before I came** to school, I had eaten my breakfast.
3. **After we had reached home,** we went to bed.
4. **While (On) opening** the door, I heard a bell ringing.
5. **After mounting** the donkey, they continued their journey.
6. **On writing his exercise,** he went home.
7. Karam had gone home, **before succeeding.**
8. You have much to do **before you depart.**
9. He departed **after he had succeeded.**
10. **When (As soon as)** I saw him, I ran.
11. **During his absence,** they played.
12. I shall wait **for your return.**
13. I have not seen him, **since his return (on returning).**
14. I fell senseless and **on becoming conscious again,** I was laying in bed.
15. **In the cat's absence,** the mice play.
16. **During their settlement,** the weather turned nasty.
17. **On hearing the child's moan,** he telephoned the doctor to come.
18. **As soon as the teacher entered,** the pupils sat down quietly.
19. He refused to say anything **when she was present.**

20. **While I was looking** out of the window, I saw Ali coming.

Exercise 73:-

1. I **should** buy a motor-car.
2. He helps you.
3. I shall throw you away.
4. She **will** not see her father.
5. He **would have failed.**
6. He would learn his lessons.
7. He **would have failed.**
8. **Will** catch the train.
9. **Should laugh.**
10. Many men **would have been killed.**
11. **Will be beaten.**
12. We shall give him a reward.
13. The master **would** send him away.
14. **Would have met his friend.**
15. **We shall not give them money.**
16. **The pupil did not apologize.**
17. **You will go on a camel.**
18. **He would have helped the poor.**
19. **The police would put him in prison.**
20. **They would enjoy sliding on ice.**
21. **He would win the match.**
22. **If he had apologized.**
23. **He would pay his debt.**
24. **He would understand the lesson.**
25. **I should have visited him.**

Exercise 74:-

1. **But for being lazy,** he would have passed easily.
2. **Without your speech,** I shall leave the room.
3. **But for trying harder,** he will fail.
4. **Unless you do this,** you will get into trouble.
5. **For raining,** we should stay indoors.
6. **If the weather is fine,** I shall go to the match.
7. **Unless he is free** he can tell nothing.
8. **If he permitted me or not,** I should go.
9. **With failure** his father will punish him.
10. **If you had not helped him,** he would have drowned.
11. **Unless we have money,** we cannot travel to Europe.
12. We cannot live **if we have not food.**
13. **Without our help,** he would have died of hunger.
14. **But for doing this, you will not get a reward.**
15. **For being careful,** you will avoid many mistakes.
16. **With or without his permission,** I shall leave the room.
17. He would be thankful, **for being helped in all his troubles.**
18. **With his confession,** he will be set free.
19. **For writing her exercise carefully,** Mary would have taken a good mark.
20. **But for obeying your mother,** she will become angry with you.

Exercise 75:-

1. **I order you.**
2. **He had been a leader.**
3. **It were a mountain.**
4. **He had been a thief.**
5. **She had been a donkey.**

Exercise 76:-

1. He held the pen **as the teacher instructed him.**
2. He entered the hall **as if be had been a king.**
3. **As the orders of the police are,** you must not leave your car in this place.
4. **As he had good luck,** he escaped punishment.
5. He walked **as if he had been a leader.**
6. Karam fought **as though he had been a lion.**
7. Everything happened **according to my hopes.**
8. The house was built **according to his orders.**
9. Mary cooks **as her mother cooks.**
10. The carpenter **looked like a skilful man in working.**

Exercise 77:-

1. He cannot answer it.
2. He became well.
3. I might see the zoo.
4. I should have not failed.
5. We shall thank you.
6. He might understand the lesson.
7. Than he forgot it.
8. You should miss the train.
9. It should fall down on the people.
10. Than the train departed.
11. The more he succeeds.
12. We might gain much money from them.
13. I had eaten my dinner.
14. The more you become fat.
15. That he could answer any question.
16. Than he awoke.
17. We believed him.

18. The more quickly you become ruined.
19. He will recover his health quickly.
20. He will become ruined.
21. He would have not been able to buy goods.
22. The manager will not employ him.
23. He has passed many laws.
24. That the porter cannot carry it.
25. She would have avoided troubles.

Exercise 78:-

1. No sooner had he found his watch than he lost it again.
2. **Had I** felt hungry, I should have eaten something.
3. **If** he **does not** try harder, he will fail.
4. **Although he was ill,** he came to school.
5. **No sooner we got** into the train, **than it began to move.**
6. **However wealthy** he is, he is unhappy.
7. **In spite of being clean,** he caught illness.
8. **No sooner had she** covered him, **than** she heard a knock on the door.
9. **In spite of my help to her,** she did not finish her work.
10. **No sonner had he** entered the room, **than the** lights went out.
11. **So lazy was he** that he could not work.
12. **Unless he was brave,** he would run away.
13. So real to me **have they** become, that I regard them as my personal friends.
14. **Although he was stupid,** he succeeded.
15. **Such a polite man is he,** that we all like him.

Exercise 79:-

1. I have not seen him **since** he came back from Europe.
2. The whole family collected **so that they might** say goodbye to their son.
3. The sportsman took up his gun **which** was lying in the corner of the hall **so that he might go** out after a tiger.
4. Lamp-black **which is one of the products obtained from coal** is used in paints and boot polishes.
5. The engineers heightened the dam **in order that they might increase our water-supply.**
6. The thief ran **so quickly that** he escaped from his pursuers.
7. **As soon as the** foundations are made, the builders begin to erect the walls.
8. **Although** the price of these motor-cars is low, we have not sold many of them.

Exercise 80:-

1. The teacher punished the pupil **who was disobedient.**
2. **When he heard that,** he became very angry.
3. The donkey began to show **that it was displeased.**
4. Some little boys marched in front **in order that they might clear the way.**
5. They met a traveller **who was walking along the** the road.
6. **Although he was ill,** he went to work as usual.
7. **Unless we have money,** we cannot buy anything.
8. **When he died,** Saladin took his place.
9. Ali was **so ill that he could not move.**

10. Everybody liked him **because he was grateful to his parents.**

11. **Although I warned him,** he carried out the journey.

12. **When he appeared,** he was shot.

13. **When they saw us,** they refused to come into the room.

14. Ali saw a ball **which was flying** in the sky.

15. The servant found his master **who was murdered** in his bed.

16. **Because he was lucky,** he escaped punishment.

17. **When they heard the tale,** they went to sleep.

18. **Although he advised them,** they went on the journey.

19. **Because the man had no money to buy food,** the man slept without supper.

20. I could make out who was there, **although it was dark.**

Exercise 81:-

1. He answered this question **because of his intelligence.**

2. **Because of being tired,** I lay down.

3. He stayed at home **till my return.**

4. The boys saw no reason **to wait.**

5. **In spite of his bravery,** he was easily beaten.

6. Nobody respected him **because of being ignorant.**

7. **In spite of being clever,** he was not given any reward.

8. **In spite of her hard work,** she was unfortunate.

9. **In spite of assisting him,** he failed to answer correctly.

10. We all work **so as to eat.**

11. **On coming to the top of the hill,** I saw a little town below.

12. The coffee was **too hot to drink.**

Mohammed,

Stan Vardhan
Abrams